MAKING
Rag Dolls

MAKING
Rag Dolls

JUANITA CLARKE

DOVER PUBLICATIONS, INC.
NEW YORK

Published in Canada by
General Publishing Company, Ltd,
30 Lesmill Road, Don Mills,
Toronto, Ontario.

This Dover edition, first published in 1996, is an unabridged and unaltered reprint
of the work originally published by
B.T. Batsford Limited,
4 Fitzhardinge Street,
London W1H 0AH.
It is published by special arrangement with the original publisher.

Dover Publications, Inc.,
31 East 2nd Street
Mineols, N.Y. 11501

Library of Congress Cataloging-in-Publication Data

Clarke, Juanita.
    Making rag dolls / Juanita Clarke.
        p.   cm.
    ISBN 0-486-28684-3 (pbk.)
    1. Rag doll making. 2. Rag dolls. I. Title.
TT175.C54 1994
745.592'21—dc20
                                                                    95-1027
                                                                    CIP

Contents

Introduction

Hello,

Welcome to a world of dolls! The dolls in this book were designed to be either country-style interior decorations, or for children to play with (in other words, durable!). They are approximately 50 cm (20 in.) tall and have been designed with a seam that joins the head to the body, to try and avoid the 'floppy-neck-syndrome', from which so many fabric dolls seem to suffer in their old age!

As each doll has a different face, hair-style and outfit, the possible combinations are endless. By choosing your favourite face, skin colour, clothes, hair colour and style, or whether or not to add glasses or freckles, it is possible to create a truly unique and personal doll. The choice is yours.

Finally, I hope that you will be inspired to make a treasure of your own, and that it gives you much pleasure and satisfaction.

Happy sewing!

JUANITA CLARKE

Before You Begin

Throughout this book I have given detailed, easy-to-follow, step-by-step instructions, but before you begin you should read through this chapter carefully. I am sure you will be anxious to get started, but a few minutes preliminary reading could save you from making any timely or costly mistakes.

EQUIPMENT

Sewing machine

The dolls and their clothes can be sewn either by hand or using a basic sewing machine that has just straight stitch. Using a machine will obviously be faster, but wherever there are instructions to machine stitch in the book, you can always hand stitch if you prefer.

Needles

I recommend size 11 needles for machine sewing. You will also need sharps for hand sewing and an embroidery needle for creating the facial features.

Fabrics and thread

I have used mainly cottons for the doll's outfits. The dolls themselves are made from a mediumweight polyester/viscose fabric, although you can use cotton calico, but wash it first, in case it shrinks. The choice of fabrics is vast, so ask for advice at your fabric shop if you are not sure which to use.

Strictly speaking, cotton thread should be used for sewing cotton fabric, and man-made thread for sewing man-made fabrics; however, I find that the best choice of colours comes in the polyester/cotton mixture range, so that is what I use.

For the facial features you need embroidery thread. Choose from Anchor, DMC, or any similar weight, six-strand embroidery thread.

Stuffing

Washable, white polyester stuffing gives the best results.

Glue

Use a clear-drying or craft glue. If you're going to do a lot of gluing, a hot-glue gun makes life easier.

Other equipment

You will also need:
a ruler
a tape measure
pins (with beaded heads)
pencils
paper scissors
fabric scissors
an iron
cardboard, medium weight (like a cereal box) for making the dolls' hair
tracing or greaseproof paper

THE PATTERNS

All the pattern pieces for the dolls in this book appear in a section at the end (*page 81* onwards) and are referred to by number at the beginning of each set of making-up instructions.

The majority of the patterns are printed full size. A few are too large for the page: some of these I have drawn as 'half patterns', which should be traced on to a folded piece of tracing paper with the fold placed along the broken line of the pattern. Other large patterns have been split into two halves and, after tracing each half individually, they should be taped together to form a single pattern. Simple rectangular shapes used for skirts, aprons or frills do not have printed patterns. I have given the measurements in each case, and a pattern number to refer to for any markings, if necessary.

A 7 mm ($\frac{1}{4}$ in.) seam allowance has been included in all the patterns.

Use tracing paper or household greaseproof paper to trace out the patterns rather than cutting out the actual patterns from the book. Remember to trace out any markings that are on the patterns, and to label each pattern, so that you know to which piece of the body or outfit they belong.

If a pattern is marked 'reverse', this means that you need to cut it out twice, turning the pattern over to cut out the second piece.

The arrows on the patterns indicate in what direction the grain of the fabric should run, and when the patterns are laid on the fabric, the arrows should run parallel to the selvedge edge (the finished edge of the fabric).

Before cutting out the patterns, move them around on the fabric until they all fit. Double-check that you have all the patterns required before starting to cut.

The facial features for each doll appear at the end of the relevant set of making-up instructions, with the guidelines for embroidery. Each set of facial features appears in a box. In order to transfer the facial features to the pattern piece for the head (no. 3), first trace the pattern piece and lay it over the box, so that the centre of the baseline of the pattern lines up exactly with the centre of the bottom line of the box. Now trace the features only on to the tracing paper: they will appear in the right position on the head pattern.

Transfer the facial features on to the right side of the fabric as follows. Turn the tracing paper over and lay it on top of the fabric. Go over the lines

again on the back of the tracing paper with a soft pencil, and the tracing will come off on to the fabric. When embroidering the facial features, embroider to the *outside* of these pencil lines to ensure they cannot be seen on the finished doll.

MEASUREMENTS

Both metric and imperial measurements are given: don't mix them in the same doll.

SAFETY

As these dolls have embroidered facial features, and no glass or button eyes that can be pulled off, they are ideal for very young children. When choosing dolls' outfits for children under three years of age, avoid those with buttons, fasteners or other small pieces that could come off. Also, if your child is too young to dress and undress the dolls, it makes sense to hand sew the bodice openings closed, rather than use fasteners. You can always sew on the fasteners sometime in the future.

Another point to remember is that when pins are used to pin the hair into position, they can get covered up and hidden. Use pins with a beaded head that will be seen more easily, and try to keep a count of the numbers of pins you have used, so you will know instantly if you have forgotten to remove one.

ABBREVIATIONS ON DIAGRAMS

RS means the right side of the fabric.
WS means the wrong side of the fabric.

STITCHES

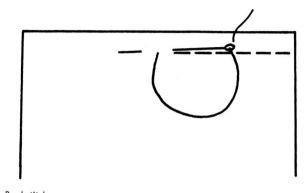

Backstitch

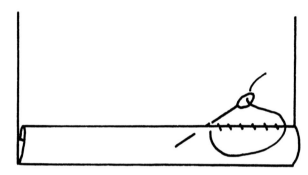

Hem stitch

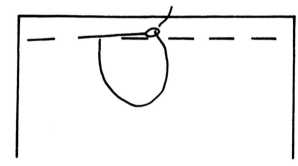

Gathering (running) stitch

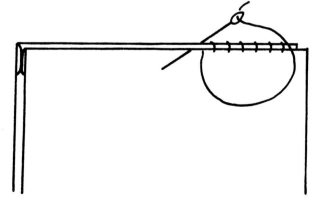

Oversewing

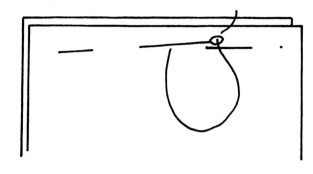

Tacking (basting)

Satin stitch

Attaching elastic

There are two methods of attaching elastic: by machine or by hand.

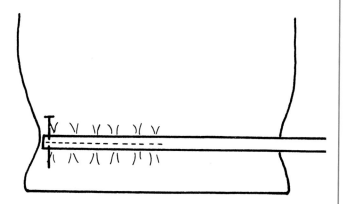

Attaching elastic by machine

Position the piece of elastic and secure it at one end with a pin. Machine stitch along the centre of the elastic, stretching the elastic as you stitch.

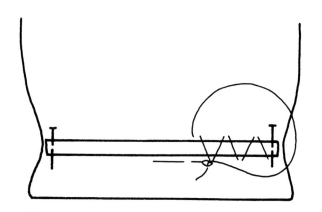

Attaching elastic by hand

Zigzag stitch along the length of elastic, stitching into the fabric.

Clipping curves

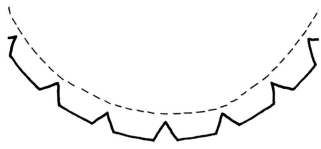

Clip the curved edges up to the stitching line. This allows the fabric to stretch around the curve smoothly.

The Doll

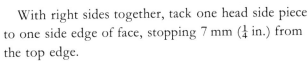

MATERIALS

40 cm (16 in.) of 115 cm (44 in.) wide fabric
454g (1lb) of stuffing

PATTERNS

arm-no. 1   head side-no. 4
leg-no. 2   body-no. 5
head-no. 3

INSTRUCTIONS

Head

Transfer the facial features to the right side of one head section (no. 3) and embroider the face following the instructions on *pages 8–9*.

With right sides together, tack one head side piece to one side edge of face, stopping 7 mm ($\frac{1}{4}$ in.) from the top edge.

With right sides together, tack the back of the head in place along the other edge of the side piece.

Tack the second side piece in place in the same way. Machine stitch all the side seams. Stitch across the top of the head along the seam allowance. Turn right side out.

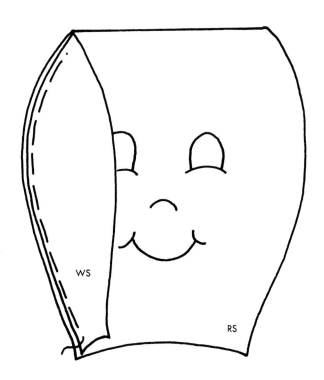

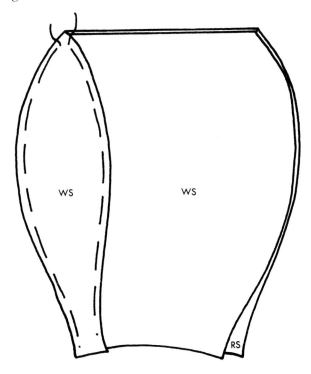

Arms

With right sides together, fold the arm in half lengthways and machine stitch along the seam allowance, leaving open at the top and between the dots. Clip curves. Turn arm right side out and repeat for the other arm.

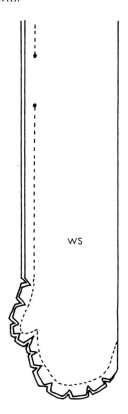

WS

Make a pleat at the top of the arm and tack in place. Pin the arms to the body front between the dots at the shoulders. (Thumbs should be pointing upwards.) Tack in place.

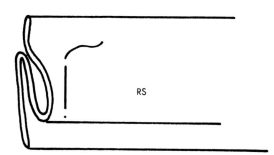

RS

Legs

With right sides together, fold each leg in half lengthways and stitch along the seam allowance, leaving open at the top and between the dots. Clip curves. Turn right side out. Bring the seam to centre front of the leg and tack across the top.

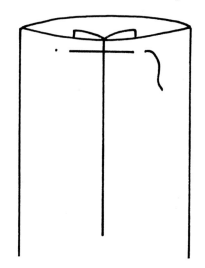

Pin the legs to the body front between the dots, toes pointing towards the body. Tack in place.

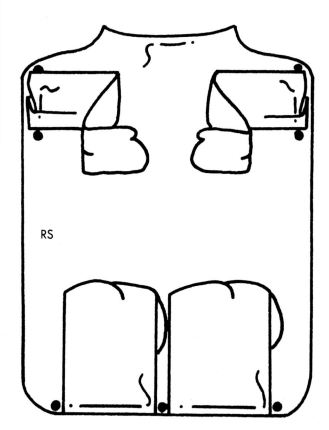

RS

With a contrasting colour thread, tack one stitch at the neck opening on the body front, to remind you that this is the front when you come to sew on the head.

Pin the body back to the body front (right sides together). Stitch, leaving open at the top and at one side for stuffing. Be careful when stitching that you do not catch the fabric of the arms and legs. Clip curves.

With right sides together, insert the head into the neck opening. Make sure that the face points to the front. Tack in position and stitch.

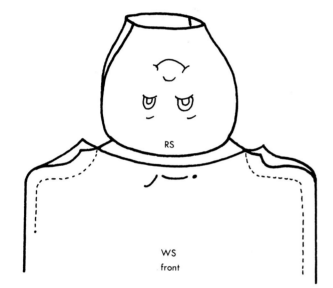

Turn the doll right side out. Stuff the head and body firmly, especially the neck area. Take time doing this, as a doll that has been slowly and carefully stuffed has a much better finished appearance. It is better to use many small pieces of stuffing than big handfuls. Hand stitch the body opening closed.

Stuff the arms and legs firmly to the gathering line. Use a blunt pencil or a knitting needle to push some stuffing carefully into the thumbs. Using a double thread and a small running stitch, stitch along the gathering line. Pull up the thread tightly, and wrap it around the limb a few times. Put in a couple of stitches to secure. Insert the needle into the top half of the limb and bring it out at the edge of the opening. Stuff the top sections of the arms and legs lightly, and hand stitch the openings closed.

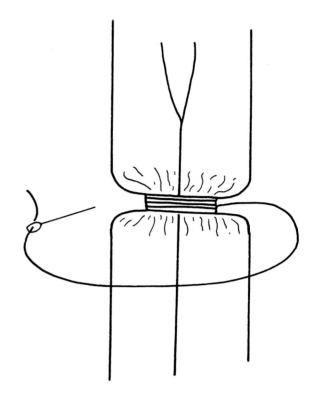

Hair

As each doll has a different hair-style, I have included the relevant instructions in each case.

Shoes and socks

Some of the dolls have shoes, or shoes and socks and the pattern pieces required are listed with their clothes.

Stitch the pieces together to form a leg shape and then follow the instructions given for the basic doll.

Nose

The nose is made by sewing a gathering stitch in a circle, close to the edge of the fabric. Pull up the gathers and insert a little stuffing into the nose. Secure the thread by putting in a few stitches, and at the same time tuck in the raw edges. Hand stitch the nose to the face.

The Basic Dress

Many of the dolls wear dresses that are variations of the basic dress pattern. These general instructions should be followed unless otherwise indicated.

INSTRUCTIONS

With right sides together, stitch the bodice front pieces to the bodice back pieces, joining at the shoulders.

With right sides together, and stretching the neck binding slightly as you work, stitch the neck binding to the bodice. Trim off any excess binding. Press under the 7 mm ($\frac{1}{4}$ in.) seam allowance on the other long edge of the binding. Fold the neck binding to the wrong side and hand stitch in place.

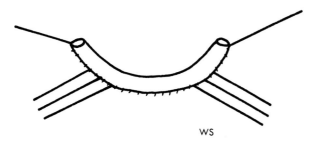

Gather the tops of the sleeves between the notches. At the bottom raw edge of the sleeves press under 7 mm ($\frac{1}{4}$ in.), then turn under another 7 mm ($\frac{1}{4}$ in.). Stitch. Attach a 13 cm (5 in.) piece of elastic, 2.5 cm (1 in.) from the finished edge of the sleeve. Pin the sleeves to the bodice, right sides together, matching the notches. Adjust the gathers evenly to fit. Stitch.

With right sides together, stitch the underarm seams of the sleeves and the bodice.

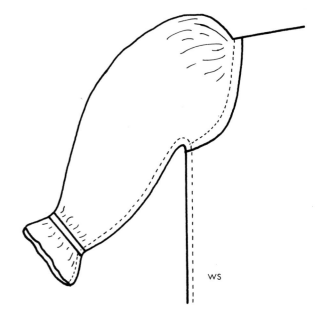

Gather the top of the skirt between the triangles, and between the square and the triangle.

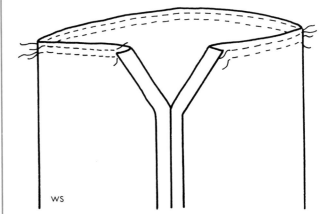

Fold the skirt in half lengthways and stitch the centre back seam, stitching from the dot down to the bottom. Press back 7 mm ($\frac{1}{4}$ in.) at the opening edge.

With right sides together, pin the skirt to the bodice. Match the bodice side seams to the triangles on the skirt and pin back the opening edges of the skirt, 7 mm ($\frac{1}{4}$ in.) in from the edge of the bodice. Pull the gathers up evenly and stitch the skirt to the bodice. Press under 7 mm ($\frac{1}{4}$ in.) at the opening edge of the bodice, and stitch from the neck to the bottom of the bodice.

Press under 7 mm ($\frac{1}{4}$ in.) at the bottom of the dress. Then press under another 2.5 cm (1 in.). Stitch close to the first pressed edge.

Put the dress on the doll. Position the snap fasteners and stitch in place.

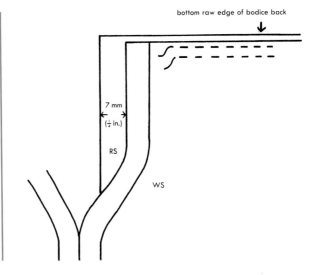

Hannah

MATERIALS

75 cm (30 in.) of 115 cm (44 in.) wide fabric for the
    dress
40 cm (16 in.) of 90 cm (36 in.) wide fabric for the
    bloomers
1 m (1 yd) of 7 mm ($\frac{1}{4}$ in.) wide elastic
craft glue
2 nylon snap fasteners
50 g (2 oz) ball of mohair yarn
1 m (1 yd) of narrow ribbon
2 ribbon roses

PATTERNS

bodice back-no. 19
bodice front-no. 18
skirt – cut one rectangle 85 cm (34 in.) × 20 cm
    (8 in.). See pattern no. 21 for markings
frill – using the dress fabric, cut three rectangles;
    two 42.5 cm (17 in.) × 6.5 cm (2$\frac{1}{2}$ in.); and one
    85 cm (34 in.) × 6.5 cm (2$\frac{1}{2}$ in.).
sleeves-no. 13
neck binding-no. 16
bloomers-no. 22 and no. 23

INSTRUCTIONS

Dress

Follow instructions for the basic dress as far as the
sewing of the underarm seams of sleeves and bodice.
    Stitch the three frill pieces together, with the
85 cm (34 in.) piece in the middle, to make one long
strip. Press under 7 mm ($\frac{1}{4}$ in.) at the bottom raw
edge of the frill, and then press under another 7 mm
($\frac{1}{4}$ in.). Stitch. Gather the top edge of the frill. With

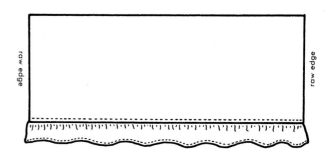

right sides together, pull up the gathers evenly and
tack the frill to the bottom raw edge of the main
skirt piece. Stitch in place.
    After attaching the frill, press lightly along the
bottom edge of the skirt and the top of the frill.
Stitch along the bottom edge of the skirt, close to
the edge.
    Gather the top of the skirt and complete the dress,
following the instructions given for the basic dress
(except for the hem).

Bloomers

Stitch centre-front crotch seam. Press under 7 mm ($\frac{1}{4}$ in.) at top edge, then press under another 13 mm ($\frac{1}{2}$ in.). Stitch in place. Thread a 32.5 cm (13 in.) piece of elastic through this casing, and secure at both ends.

Press under 7 mm ($\frac{1}{4}$ in.) at bottom edges of bloomers, then press under another 7 mm ($\frac{1}{4}$ in.). Stitch in place. Attach a 14 cm ($5\frac{1}{2}$ in.) piece of elastic, 2 cm ($\frac{3}{4}$ in.) in from each finished edge.

Stitch centre-back crotch seam. Stitch inside leg seams. Turn right side out. Stitch a ribbon rose to the bottom of each leg at the sides.

Hair

Make two.

Cut a piece of cardboard 18 cm (7 in.) long by at least 25 cm (10 in.) wide. Wind the mohair yarn lengthways around the cardboard, until you have a mat of yarn, no more than 25 cm (10 in.) wide. Backstitch a seam, keeping the strands pushed up closely together, using matching coloured thread, across the 25 cm (10 in.).

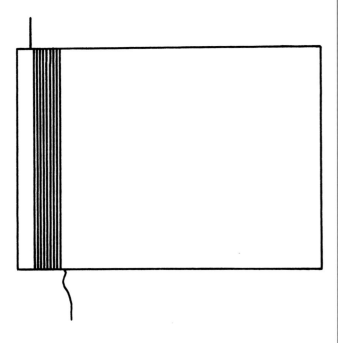

Cut across the yarn, making sure that the seam is in the centre. Machine stitch along the backstitched seam, using tissue paper above and below so the yarn does not get caught in the machine.

Tear off the tissue paper carefully.

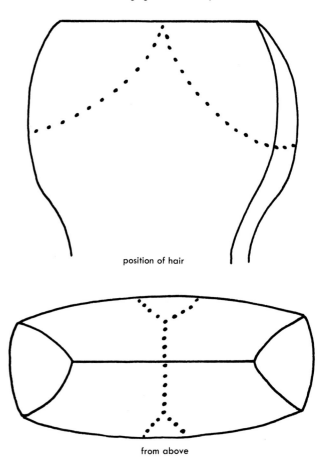

position of hair

from above

Pin the hair pieces to the head. The two edges should join at the top to form a circle. Push them tightly together, or overlap slightly. When you are satisfied with the position of the hair, spread some glue underneath the hair piece along the hair seamline, using the pins to prevent the hair moving around. Finally, while the glue is still wet, hand stitch the hair to the head. Remove the pins before the glue dries completely.

Tie the hair up into bunches with a spare piece of yarn, and finish off with ribbon bows.

EMBROIDERY

Mouth: use two strands of pink, in small backstitches.

Nose: use two strands of light brown, in small backstitches.

Glasses: use two strands of dark grey, in small backstitches.

Eyelids: use two strands of light brown, in small backstitches.

Eyelashes: use one strand of light brown, in individual long stitches.

Small circle in the eye: use two strands of white, in satin stitch.

Pupil of the eye: use two strands of black, in satin stitch.

Inner area of the iris: use two strands of dark brown, in satin stitch.

Outer area of the iris: use two strands of light brown, in satin stitch.

Willow

MATERIALS

60 cm (24 in.) of 115 cm (44 in.) wide fabric for the
    dress and bow
60 cm (24 in.) of 115 cm. (44 in.) wide fabric for the
    bloomers and apron
23 cm (9 in.) of 35 mm ($1\frac{1}{2}$ in.) wide pre-gathered lace
1 m (1 yd) of 7 mm ($\frac{1}{4}$ in.) elastic
craft glue
1 m (1 yd) of narrow ribbon
3 nylon snap fasteners
50 g (2 oz) ball of cotton yarn

PATTERNS

bodice back-no. 15
bodice front-no. 14
skirt – cut one rectangle 110 cm (44 in.) × 25 cm
    (10 in.). See pattern no. 24 for markings
sleeves-no. 13
neck binding-no. 16
bloomers-no. 22 and no. 23
apron – cut one rectangle 53 cm (21 in.) × 20 cm
    (8 in.)
apron waist band-no. 25
bow – cut a 9 cm ($3\frac{1}{2}$ in.) square of fabric, and a
    rectangle 5 cm (2 in.) × 4.5 cm ($1\frac{3}{4}$ in.)

INSTRUCTIONS

Dress
With right sides together, stitch the bodice front
pieces to the bodice back pieces at the shoulders.
Tack the lace around the raw edge of the neck.

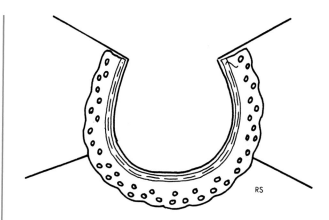

With right sides together, stretching the neck
binding slightly as you work, stitch the neck binding
to the bodice. Trim off any excess binding or lace.

Complete, following the instructions for the basic
dress (*page 14*).

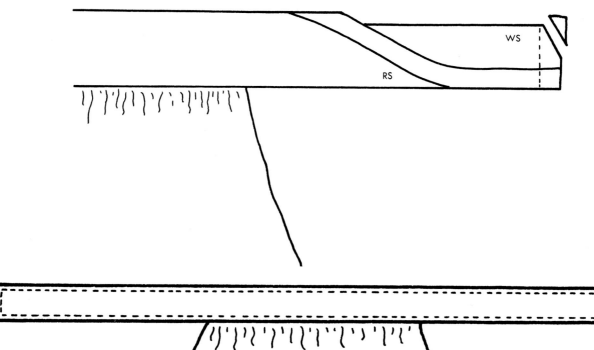

Apron

Press under 7 mm (¼ in.) along the sides of the apron, then press under another 7 mm (¼ in.). Stitch.

Press under 7 mm (¼ in.) along bottom edge, then press under another 2 cm (¾ in.). Stitch.

Gather across the top edge of the apron and, with right sides together, pin to the waist band between the dots. Adjust the gathers evenly, and stitch.

Press the seam allowance towards the waist band continuing to press right up to the ends of the waist band.

Press under 7 mm (¼ in.) along the other long edge of the waist band. Fold the waist band in half lengthways, right sides together. Stitch the ends and clip the corners.

Turn the waist band right side out. Stitch along both edges of the waist band.

Bow

Fold the square of fabric in half, right sides together, and machine along one short side and the long side. Turn right side out. Fold in the raw edges of the short side and hand stitch the opening closed.

To make the band, fold the rectangle in half lengthways and machine along the 5 cm (2 in.) side. Turn right side out and press.

Gather the bow up in the centre and wrap the band around it. Stitch the band to the bow, at the back of the bow, trimming the band to fit.

Using small running stitches, gather a line, 5 cm (2 in.) long, up from the bottom edge of the apron and secure. This line should be approximately 10 cm (4 in.) to one side of the centre of the apron.

Gather the apron to pull it up in one spot and sew the bow to the apron at the top of this gathered line.

Bloomers

Follow the instructions given for Hannah's bloomers (*page 18*).

Hair

Using a piece of cardboard 50 cm (20 in.) long by at least 9 cm (3½ in.) wide, follow the instructions given for Hannah's hair (*page 18*) (making the mat of yarn 9 cm (3½ in.) wide). Glue or stitch the hair on to the doll's head and tie it up into two bunches using a spare piece of yarn.

When you have made your bunches, divide each into three and plait. Tie the ends securely.

Bring the ends up to form loops and tie in place.

Stitch or glue the loops to the side of the head.

Make two bows from the ribbon, and stitch or glue them in place.

EMBROIDERY

Mouth: use two strands of pink, in satin stitch.

Nose: use two strands of light brown, in a single stitch.

Eyebrows and the line around the eye: use two strands of light brown, in small backstitches.

Eyelashes: use one strand of light brown, in individual stitches.

Pupil of the eye: use two strands of black, in satin stitch.

Small circle in the eye: use two strands of white, in satin stitch.

Inner area of the iris: use two strands of medium brown, in satin stitch.

Outer area of the iris: use two strands of light brown, in satin stitch.

Tillie

MATERIALS

50 cm (20 in.) of 115 cm (44 in.) wide fabric for the dress
30 cm (12 in.) of 90 cm (36 in.) wide fabric for the bloomers
1 m (1 yd) of 7 mm ($\frac{1}{4}$ in.) elastic
craft glue
3 nylon snap fasteners
50 g (2 oz) ball of cotton yarn
approximately 20 beads for the hair

PATTERNS

bodice back-no. 19
bodice front-no. 18
sleeves-no. 13
skirt – cut one rectangle 110 cm (44 in.) × 25 cm (10 in.). See pattern no. 24 for markings
neck binding-no. 16
bloomers-no. 22 and no. 26

INSTRUCTIONS

Dress
Follow the instructions given for the basic dress.

Bloomers
Follow the instructions given for Hannah's bloomers (*page 18*).

Hair
Make two.

Using a piece of cardboard 22 cm ($8\frac{3}{4}$ in.) long by at least 18 cm (7 in.) wide, follow the instructions given for Hannah's hair (*page 18*) (making the mat of yarn 18 cm (7 in.) wide), as far as having torn off the tissue paper.

Glue or stitch the hair on to the head with the seams running from side to side rather than from back to front. One of the hair pieces falls to the front, the other to the back.

Make plaits in the hair, securing their ends by tying tightly with thread of a matching colour. When plaiting at the sides, use some strands from the back and some strands from the front.

Trim the plaits at the front to form the fringe.

Thread the plaits through the hair beads and either sew or glue the beads on.

EMBROIDERY

Mouth: use two strands of red, in satin stitch.

Nose, eyebrows and the lines under and around the top of the eye: use two strands of black, in small backstitches.

Pupil of the eye: use two strands of black, in satin stitch.

Small circle in the eye: use two strands of white, in satin stitch.

Iris of the eye: use two strands of medium brown, in satin stitch.

Outer area of the eye: use two strands of white, in satin stitch.

Sandy

MATERIALS

40 cm (16 in.) of 115 cm (44 in.) wide fabric for the
dungarees and the cap
40 cm (16 in.) of 115 cm (44 in.) wide fabric for the
shirt
50 cm (20 in.) of 7 mm ($\frac{1}{4}$ in.) wide elastic
3 nylon snap fasteners
small ball of cotton yarn
craft glue

PATTERNS

bodice back-no. 28
bodice front-no. 27
sleeves-no. 13
neck binding-no. 16
dungaree trousers-no. 29 and no. 30
dungaree bib-no. 31
dungaree pocket-no. 32
dungaree shoulder straps-no. 33
cap-no. 36
cap band-no. 34
cap peak-no. 35

INSTRUCTIONS

Shirt

With right sides together, stitch the shoulder seams.
Sew on the neck binding and attach the sleeves
following the instructions given for the basic dress.

At the bottom raw edge of the sleeves, press
under 7 mm ($\frac{1}{4}$ in.), then press under another 7 mm
($\frac{1}{4}$ in.). Stitch.

Attach a 13 cm (5 in.) piece of elastic, 2.5 cm
(1 in.) in from the finished edge of the sleeve.

With right sides together, stitch the underarm
seams of the sleeves and the bodice.

Press under 7 mm ($\frac{1}{4}$ in.) at each opening edge.
Machine stitch along the edge, keeping close to the
edge.

Press under 7 mm ($\frac{1}{4}$ in.), then press under another
13 mm ($\frac{1}{2}$ in.) at the bottom of the shirt. Stitch. Sew
on the snap fasteners.

Dungarees

Press under 7 mm ($\frac{1}{4}$ in.) around the dungaree pocket
and stitch all the way round, keeping close to the
edge. Stitch in position on the dungaree bib.

Press under 7 mm ($\frac{1}{4}$ in.) along the two long sides
of the bib. With wrong sides together, fold along
the top fold line. Stitch along each side and along
the top of the bib, keeping close to the edge.

Sew the centre-front crotch seam. Press under
2 cm ($\frac{3}{4}$ in.) along the top edge of the trousers. Pin
the bib to the centre-front, with the raw edge of the
bib 7 mm ($\frac{1}{4}$ in.) below the fold at the top of the
trousers. Stitch along the fold, close to the edge.

Attach a 9.5 cm ($3\frac{3}{4}$ in.) piece of elastic to each
side on the back of the trousers.

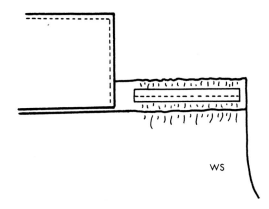

WS

With right sides together, stitch the back crotch seam and then the inside leg seams. Turn the dungarees right side out and fold the fabric up 13 mm ($\frac{1}{2}$ in.), then fold up another 13 mm ($\frac{1}{2}$ in.) to make the turn-ups.

With right sides together, fold the shoulder straps in half. Stitch along the long edge. Turn right side out. (If a heavy fabric has been used the seam allowance may need to be trimmed to make it easier to turn right side out.)

Attach the straps to the back of the dungarees and to the front corners of the bib, crossing them over at the back. (If the doll is going to be dressed and undressed, you might prefer to attach the straps to the front with snap fasteners.)

Cap

Press under 7 mm ($\frac{1}{4}$ in.) along one long edge of the band. Stitch. With right sides together, stitch the short edges together to form a circular band. With right sides together, pin the band to the circle of fabric, easing to fit. Stitch. Turn right side out.

With right sides together, stitch around the curved edge of the cap peak. Clip curves, turn right side out and press. Stitch to the centre front of the cap.

Position on the doll's head and secure with a few hand stitches.

Hair

Make approximately ten bunches.

Wrap the yarn around three fingers eight times. Secure by tying with another piece of yarn and a double knot. Glue or stitch the hair in place around the edge of the cap.

EMBROIDERY

Mouth and nose: use two strands of pink, in small backstitches.

Line around the eye: use two strands of dark grey, in small backstitches.

Eyelashes: use one strand of dark grey, in small backstitches.

Pupil of the eye: use two strands of dark grey, in satin stitch.

Small circle in the eye: use two strands of white, in satin stitch.

Inner area of the iris: use two strands of dark blue, in satin stitch.

Middle area of the iris: use two strands of medium blue, in satin stitch.

Outer area of the iris: use two strands of light blue, in satin stitch.

Victoria

MATERIALS

50 cm (20 in.) of 115 cm (44 in.) wide fabric for the dress

30 cm (12 in.) of 115 cm (44 in.) wide fabric for the bloomers and the bib

1 m (1 yd) of 7 mm ($\frac{1}{4}$ in.) wide elastic

craft glue

3 nylon snap fasteners

50 g (2 oz) ball of cotton yarn

50 cm (20 in.) of narrow ribbon

PATTERNS

bodice front-no. 37

bodice back-no. 38

neck binding-no. 16

bib-no. 39

sleeves-no. 13

skirt – cut two rectangles of fabric, each measuring 56 cm (22 in.) × 16 cm ($6\frac{1}{4}$ in.)

bloomers-no. 22 and no. 26

INSTRUCTIONS

Dress

With right sides of bib together, stitch the side seams. Trim the corners, turn right side out and press.

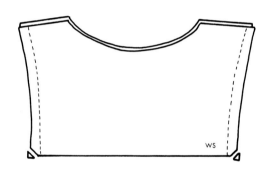

Tack the bib to the bodice front.

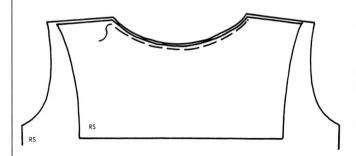

Complete the bodice section and attach the sleeves following the instructions given for the basic dress.

At the bottom raw edge of the sleeve, press under 7 mm ($\frac{1}{4}$ in.) then press under another 13 mm ($\frac{1}{2}$ in.). Stitch. Thread a 13 cm (5 in.) piece of elastic through this casing, and secure at each end.

Press under 7 mm ($\frac{1}{4}$ in.) at bodice backs. Stitch. Overlap the two back opening pieces 13 mm ($\frac{1}{2}$ in.) and tack the two pieces together.

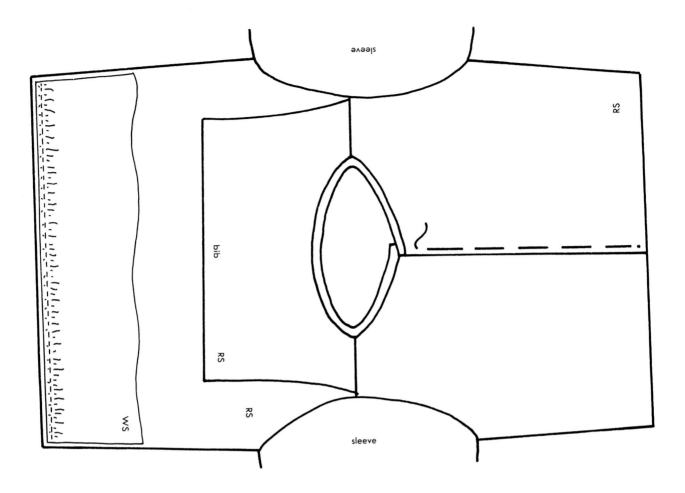

Gather up the top edges of both skirt sections to fit the bodice front and back. Sew the skirts to bodice front and back.

With right sides of fabric together, stitch underarm, side and skirt seams.

Press under 7 mm ($\frac{1}{4}$ in.) then press under another 2.5 cm (1 in.) at the bottom of the skirt. Stitch. Sew on the snap fasteners.

Bloomers

Sew the bloomers following the instructions given for Hannah's bloomers (*page 18*)

Hair

Using a piece of cardboard 3.5 cm ($1\frac{1}{2}$ in.) long by at least 12 cm ($4\frac{3}{4}$ in.) wide, follow the instructions given for Hannah's hair (*page 18*) (making the mat of yarn 12 cm ($4\frac{3}{4}$ in.) wide), as far as having torn off the tissue paper.

Make another mat of hair, measuring 9 cm ($3\frac{1}{2}$ in.) × 50 cm (20 in.).

Glue or stitch the fringe across the front of the head. Glue or stitch the main hair piece on top of the head, overlapping the fringe seam, with the seam running from front to back.

Leave approximately 10 cm (4 in.) at the top unplaited, then plait the rest. Trim to the desired length and tie securely, using a piece of thread.

Glue or stitch the top of the plaits to the side of the head.

Tie some ribbon on to the ends of the plaits.

EMBROIDERY

Mouth: use two strands of pink, in satin stitch.

Nose: use two strands of pink, in a single stitch.

Eyebrows and eyelids: use two strands of dark grey, in small backstitches.

Eyelashes: use one strand of dark grey, in small backstitches.

Pupil of the eye: use two strands of black, in satin stitch.

Small circle in the eye: use two strands of white, in satin stitch.

Inner area of the iris: use two strands of dark green, in satin stitch.

Middle area of the iris: use two strands of medium green, in satin stitch.

Outer area of the iris: use two strands of light green, in satin stitch.

Katie

MATERIALS

60 cm (24 in.) of 115 cm (44 in.) wide fabric for the nightie

10 cm (4 in.) of 115 cm (44 in.) wide fabric for the slippers

Two 18 cm (7 in.) square pieces of felt for the teddy

25 cm (10 in.) of 7 mm ($\frac{1}{4}$ in.) elastic

3 nylon snap fasteners

3 buttons

50 g (2 oz) ball of cotton yarn

craft glue

PATTERNS

bodice back-no. 14

bodice front-no. 15

sleeves-no. 13

neck binding-no. 16

teddy-no. 40

slippers-no. 41

skirt – cut two rectangles 46 × 29 cm (18 × 11$\frac{1}{2}$ in.)

INSTRUCTIONS

Nightie

Stitch bodice back to bodice fronts, sew on neck binding and attach sleeves, following the instructions given for the basic dress.

At the bottom raw edge of the sleeves, press under 7 mm ($\frac{1}{4}$ in.) then press under another 13 mm ($\frac{1}{2}$ in.). Stitch. Thread 13 cm (5 in.) of elastic through this casing and secure at each end.

Press under 7 mm ($\frac{1}{4}$ in.) at the bodice opening edges. Stitch. Overlap the opening edges by 13 mm ($\frac{1}{2}$ in.) and tack together.

Complete the nightie following the instructions given for Victoria's dress (*page 30*).

Stitch the snap fasteners along the front opening, spacing them evenly.

Sew the buttons on to the front of the nightie.

Slippers

If you are using fur fabric, you may find it easier to sew the slippers by hand.

First, fold 7 mm ($\frac{1}{4}$ in.) over to the wrong side, along the two top straight edges. Stitch.

Fold the slipper in half, with right sides together, and backstitch along the diagonal line.

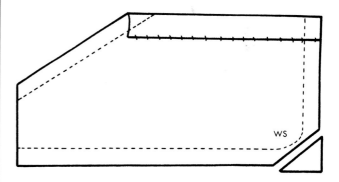

Stitch along the bottom and back of the slipper, curving at the heel. Trim the seam allowance, if necessary, and turn right side out.

Teddy

Embroider the facial features on to one of the felt pieces.

With wrong sides together, and using a small running stitch, hand stitch around the teddy, leaving an opening for the stuffing. Stuff the teddy and hand stitch the opening closed. Stitch lines inside the ears.

Hair

Make approximately 30 bunches.

Wrap the yarn around three fingers 15 times, and secure by tying with another piece of yarn.

Glue or stitch the bunches of yarn on to the head.

EMBROIDERY

Mouth: use two strands of pink, in small backstitches.

Freckles: use two strands of light brown, in a single stitch.

Nose, the line around the outside of the eye and the eyebrows: use two strands of light brown, in small backstitches.

Eyelashes: use one strand of light brown, in small backstitches.

Pupil: use two strands of black, in satin stitch.

Small circle in the eye: use two strands of white, in satin stitch.

Iris: use two strands of medium brown, in satin stitch.

Poppy

MATERIALS

60 cm (24 in.) of 115 cm (44 in.) wide fabric for the
  jumpsuit
25 cm (10 in.) of 90 cm (36 in.) wide fabric for the
  bib and cuffs
15 cm (6 in.) × 10 cm (4 in.) piece of fabric for the
  bow tie
1 m (1 yd) of narrow ribbon
2 nylon snap fasteners
50 g (2 oz) ball of cotton yarn

PATTERNS

bodice front-no. 18
bodice back-no. 19
sleeves-no. 20
bib-no. 42
trousers-no. 43 and no. 44
neck binding-no. 16
cuffs – cut four rectangles 16.5 cm (6$\frac{1}{2}$ in.) × 6.5 cm
  (2$\frac{1}{2}$ in.)
bow – cut a 9 cm (3$\frac{1}{2}$ in.) square of fabric, and a
  rectangle 5 cm (2 in.) × 4.5 cm (1$\frac{3}{4}$ in.)

INSTRUCTIONS

Jumpsuit

With right sides of the two bib pieces together,
stitch along the side seams. Turn the bib right side
out and press. Stitch two pieces of ribbon, 3 mm
($\frac{1}{8}$ in.) in from each side.

Tack the bib to the bodice front. Machine stitch
the bib to the bodice front along the sides of the
bib, keeping close to the edge.

Sew the bodice backs to the bodice front and sew
on the neck binding, following the instructions
given for the basic dress.

Gather the tops of the sleeves between the notches
and sew to the bodice.

Gather the bottom edge of the sleeves.

Stitch a piece of ribbon on to the cuff.

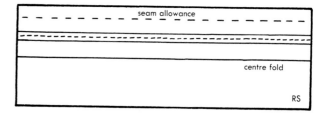

With the right sides of the cuff and the sleeve
together, stitch the cuff to the sleeve. Press under
7 mm ($\frac{1}{4}$ in.) along the other raw edge of the cuff
band.

With the right sides of the bodice and the sleeve
together, stitch the underarm and bodice side seams.

Fold over the cuff to the wrong side and hem
stitch in place.

With right sides together, stitch the side seams of
both leg sections.

Stitch the cuffs to the bottom of each leg section,
following the instructions given for the armbands,
and making sure that the leg side seam is in the
centre of the cuff.

Press under 7 mm ($\frac{1}{4}$ in.) along each long side of
the cuff. Stitch one crotch seam (front) to join the
two leg sections together.

Gather across the top of the legs in three sections:

First across one back piece, starting 2 cm ($\frac{3}{4}$ in.) in
from the back opening edge

Secondly across the two front pieces

Thirdly across the remaining back piece, stopping 2 cm ($\frac{3}{4}$ in.) in from the edge.

Stitch the back crotch seam, stopping 7.5 cm (3 in.) from the top. With right sides together, stitch the leg section to the bodice, matching the side seams and having the centre front crotch seam at the centre of the bodice, adjusting gathers to fit.

Press under 7 mm ($\frac{1}{4}$ in.) along the back opening edges. Stitch from the neck down to the bottom of the bodice, stitching close to the edge.

Stitch the inside leg seams.

Fold the cuffs to the wrong side and hem stitch in place.

Stitch two snap fasteners to the bodice back opening.

Make the bow by folding the square of fabric in half. Machine stitch along one short side and the long side. Turn right side out and press. Fold in the raw edges of the short side and hand stitch the opening closed.

Make a band by folding the rectangle of fabric in half lengthways and machine stitching along the 5 cm (2 in.) side. Turn right side out and press.

Gather the bow up in the centre and wrap the band around it. Stitch the band to the bow, at the back of the bow, trimming the band to fit.

Stitch the bow to the front of the bodice at the neck.

Hair

Make approximately 40 bunches.

Wrap the yarn around four fingers, ten times. Tie another piece of yarn around to secure. Snip the yarn opposite the tie. Glue or stitch the bunches of yarn on to the head.

EMBROIDERY

Mouth: use two strands of pink, in satin stitch for the hearts and in backstitch for the line.

Nose: use two strands of pink, in satin stitch.

Eyelashes and around the outer circle of the eye: use two strands of dark grey, in small backstitches.

Pupil of the eye: use two strands of dark grey, in satin stitch.

Small circle in the eye: use two strands of white, in satin stitch.

Iris: use two strands of medium grey, in satin stitch.

Outer circle of the eye: use two strands of white, in satin stitch.

Chelsea

MATERIALS

60 cm (24 in.) of 115 cm (44 in.) wide fabric for the
  dress
25 cm (10 in.) of 115 cm (44 in.) wide fabric for the
  petticoat
40 cm (16 in.) of 90 cm (36 in.) wide fabric for the
  bloomers and the bows
1 m (1 yd) of 4.5 cm ($1\frac{3}{4}$ in.) wide lace
23 cm (9 in.) of 3.5 cm ($1\frac{1}{2}$ in.) wide pre-gathered lace
1 m (1 yd) of 7 mm ($\frac{1}{4}$ in.) wide elastic
50 g (2 oz) ball of cotton yarn
3 nylon snap fasteners
craft glue

PATTERNS

bodice front-no. 18
bodice back-no. 19
sleeve-no. 13
neck binding-no. 16
skirt – cut one rectangle 95 cm (38 in.) × 29 cm
  ($11\frac{1}{2}$ in.)
petticoat – cut one rectangle 95 cm (38 in.) × 25 cm
  (10 in.)
bloomers-no. 22 and no. 23

INSTRUCTIONS

Dress

Complete the bodice and sleeves following the
instructions given for Willow's dress (*page 21*).

   Machine stitch the lace to one raw edge of the
petticoat.

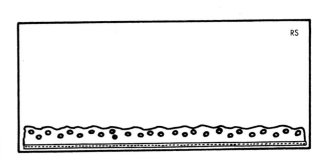

Fold the lace down flat and press the seam allowance
towards the back of the petticoat. Machine stitch
along the folded bottom edge of the petticoat to
hold the lace down.

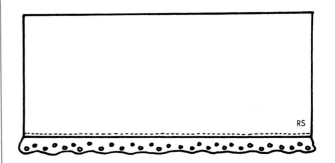

   Place the rectangle of skirt fabric on top of the
petticoat, with the wrong side of the skirt fabric on
the right side of the petticoat.

   Tack the two pieces together along the top edge.
Gather along the top raw edge in three sections:

   First gather for 22.5 cm (9 in.), starting 2 cm ($\frac{3}{4}$ in.)
in from the edge.

   Secondly gather for 46 cm ($18\frac{1}{2}$ in.).

   Thirdly gather for 22.5 cm (9 in.), ending 2 cm
($\frac{3}{4}$ in.) before the end.

   Sew the back seams of the skirt and the petticoat,
starting 5 cm (2 in.) down from the top and stitching
to the bottom.

Hem the skirt by pressing under 7 mm ($\frac{1}{4}$ in.), then under another 2.5 cm (1 in.). Stitch.

Machine stitch the skirt section to the bodice, adjusting gathers to fit, and matching the side seams of the bodice to the breaks in the gathering.

Press under 7 mm ($\frac{1}{4}$ in.) along each bodice back opening. Stitch from the top to the bottom of each bodice back opening, keeping close to the edge.

Place the dress on the doll and position the snap fasteners. Remove the dress and hand sew the fasteners on.

Make two bows, following the instructions given for Willow's bow (*page 22*).

Attach one bow to the front of the dress, following the instructions given for Willow's apron (*page 22*). Sew the bow to the doll's head after the hair has been put on.

Hair

Using a piece of cardboard 12.5 cm (5 in.) long by at least 20 cm (8 in.) wide, follow the instructions given for Hannah's hair (*page 18*) (making a mat of yarn 17 cm ($6\frac{3}{4}$ in.) wide, as far as having torn off the tissue paper.

Using a second piece of cardboard, 5 cm (2 in.) long by 25 cm (10 in.) wide, make a mat of yarn 20 cm (8 in.) wide. Finish in the same way as the previous hair piece.

Using that same piece of cardboard make another mat of yarn 19 cm ($7\frac{1}{2}$ in.) wide. Finish in the same way as the first hair piece. This last piece is the fringe.

Fold the fringe in half along the 19 cm ($7\frac{1}{2}$ in.). Place the fringe on the head, 1 cm ($\frac{3}{8}$ in.) to the front of the seam, on the top of the head. The fringe will fall about a third of the way down each side of the head. Pin in place.

Fold the first hair piece in half and butt the seam up to the seam of the fringe. Pin in place.

Place the other hair piece around the back of the head, going from one side of the face to the other. It is important not to allow the pieces to stretch. Pin in place.

As different weights of yarn will fall differently, you may need to fiddle with the hair until you are happy that it looks good.

Glue or stitch the hair on, using the pins to help hold the hair in place. Hand stitch the main hair piece to the fringe, along the seams, while the glue is still wet.

Trim the hair into shape at the sides, and around the fringe if necessary.

EMBROIDERY

Mouth: use two strands of pink, in small backstitches.
Nose, eyelids and eyebrows: use two strands of light brown, in small backstitches.
Pupil of the eye: use two strands of black, in satin stitch.
Small circle at the top of the eye: use two strands of white, in satin stitch.
Inner area of the iris: use two strands of dark brown, in satin stitch.
Outer area of the iris: use two strands of light brown, in satin stitch.
Eyelashes: use one strand of light brown, in a single stitch.

Corey

MATERIALS

30 cm (12 in.) of 115 cm (44 in.) wide fabric for the shirt

35 cm (14 in.) of 90 cm (36 in.) wide fabric for the trousers

45 cm (18 in.) of 7 mm ($\frac{1}{4}$ in.) wide elastic

3 nylon snap fasteners

2 buttons for the trousers (optional)

small ball of yarn

craft glue

PATTERNS

bodice front-no. 38
bodice back-no. 37
sleeves-no. 46
neck binding-no. 16
trousers-no. 29 and no. 52
shoulder straps-no. 53

INSTRUCTIONS

Trousers

Stitch one crotch seam. This will be the centre-front seam.

Press under 2 cm ($\frac{3}{4}$ in.), along the top edge of the trousers. Cut two pieces of elastic 9.5 cm ($3\frac{3}{4}$ in.) long. Attach the elastic to the wrong side of the trousers, following the instructions given for Sandy's dungarees (*page 27*).

Stitch the centre-back crotch seam.

Stitch the inside leg seams.

Fold turn-ups at the bottom of each leg.

Fold the straps in half, lengthways, with right sides together. Stitch along the long raw edge. Turn right side out and press.

Stitch the slanted edge of the straps to the back of the trousers, tucking them in 7 mm ($\frac{1}{4}$ in.) below the top of the trousers.

Cross over the straps and stitch the other ends to the front of the trousers.

Sew on the buttons.

Shirt

Stitch the shoulder seams, sew on the neck binding, and attach the sleeves, following the instructions given for the basic dress.

Press under 7 mm ($\frac{1}{4}$ in.), and then press under another 13 mm ($\frac{1}{2}$ in.) at the bottom of each sleeve. Stitch. Thread a 13 cm (5 in.) piece of elastic through this casing and secure at both ends.

With right sides together, stitch the underarm and side seams.

Press under 7 mm ($\frac{1}{4}$ in) along each back opening edge. Machine stitch along the edge, keeping close to the edge.

Press under 7 mm ($\frac{1}{4}$ in.), then press under another 13 mm ($\frac{1}{2}$ in.) at the bottom of the shirt. Stitch.

Sew on the snap fasteners.

Hair

Make approximately 40 bunches.

Thread a 50 cm (20 in.) long piece of yarn on to a needle. Wrap the yarn around one finger six times. Using the needle, make a few stitches to secure.

Glue or stitch the bunches on to the head.

EMBROIDERY

Mouth: use two strands of red, in small backstitches.

Nose and the line under and around the top of the eye: use two strands of dark grey, in small backstitches.

Eyelashes: use one strand of black, in individual long stitches.

Glasses: use two strands of light brown, in small backstitches.

Pupil of the eye: use two strands of black, in satin stitch.

Small circle in the eye: use two strands of white, in satin stitch.

Inner area of the iris: use two strands of medium grey, in satin stitch.

Outer area of the iris: use two strands of light grey, in satin stitch.

Rebecca

MATERIALS

60 cm (24 in.) of 115 cm (44 in.) wide fabric for the
   dress
40 cm (16 in.) of 90 cm (36 in.) wide fabric for the
   bloomers
2 m (2 yd) of 3 cm ($1\frac{1}{4}$ in.) wide pre-gathered lace
1 m (1 yd) of 7 mm ($\frac{1}{4}$ in.) wide elastic
3 nylon snap fasteners
50 g (2 oz) ball of yarn
50 cm (20 in.) of narrow ribbon
craft glue

PATTERNS

bodice front-no. 14
bodice back-no. 15
sleeves-no. 13
neck binding-no. 16
skirt – cut one rectangle 110 cm (44 in.) × 25 cm
   (10 in.). See pattern no. 24 for markings.
pocket-no. 54
bloomers-no. 22 and no. 23

INSTRUCTIONS

Dress

Stitch the shoulder seams, sew on the lace and the
neck binding, and attach the sleeves, following the
instructions given for Willow's dress (*page 21*).

Sew a 24 cm ($9\frac{1}{2}$ in.) piece of lace to the bottom
edge of each sleeve, following the instructions given
for attaching the lace to Chelsea's petticoat (*page 40*).

Attach a 13 cm (5 in.) piece of elastic, 2.5 cm
(1 in.) in from the edge of the fabric at the bottom
of each sleeve.

With right sides together, stitch the underarm and
bodice side seams.

Cut two pieces of lace, each 20 cm (8 in.) long.

With the right sides of the lace and the pocket
together, stitch the lace around the curved edge of
the pocket.

Press the raw edge of the pocket to the wrong
side. Stitch around the curved edge of the pocket,
keeping close to the edge.

Press under 7 mm ($\frac{1}{4}$ in.) along the top raw edge.
Machine stitch across.

Stitch the pocket on to the front of the skirt.

Complete the dress following the instructions
given for the basic dress.

Bloomers

Attach a 24 cm ($9\frac{1}{2}$ in.) piece of lace to the bottom of
each leg, following the instructions given for
attaching the lace to Chelsea's petticoat (*page 40*).
Make up the bloomers, following the instructions
given for Hannah's bloomers (*page 18*).

Hair

Using a piece of cardboard 14 cm ($5\frac{1}{2}$ in.) long by at
least 35 cm (14 in.) wide, follow the instructions
given for Hannah's hair (*page 18*) (making a mat of
yarn 35 cm (14 in.) wide). Pin the hair in a circle
around the head, keeping the join to the back. Glue
or stitch the hair in place.

Tie the hair up using a spare piece of yarn and
decorate with some ribbon.

EMBROIDERY

Mouth: use two strands of red, in small backstitches.

Freckles: use two strands of light brown, in a single stitch.

Nose, eyebrows and the lines under and around the top of the eye: use two strands of dark grey, in a small backstitch.

Eyelashes: use one strand of black, in individual stitches.

Pupil of the eye: use two strands of black, in satin stitch.

Small circle in the eye: use two strands of white, in satin stitch.

Inner area of the iris: use two strands of medium grey, in satin stitch.

Outer area of the iris: use two strands of light grey, in satin stitch.

Rose

MATERIALS

40 cm (16 in.) of 115 cm (44 in.) wide fabric for the coat

15 cm (6 in.) × 10 cm (4 in.) piece of fabric for the socks

40 cm (16 in.) × 9 cm ($3\frac{1}{2}$ in.) piece of fabric for the shoes

30 cm (12 in.) of narrow, pre-gathered lace for the socks

2 nylon snap fasteners

4 small brass buttons

2 buttons for the shoes

50 g (2 oz) ball of chenille yarn

PATTERNS

coat bodice back-no. 60

coat bodice front-no. 61

coat sleeves-no. 62

coat collar-no. 63

coat skirt – cut one rectangle 70 cm (28 in.) × 26.5 cm ($10\frac{1}{2}$ in.) (or the desired length to suit any dress you may have made for her).

leg-no. 7

ankle sock-no. 12

shoe-no. 11

INSTRUCTIONS

Coat

Stitch the bodice fronts to the bodice back at the shoulders.

Press under 3 mm ($\frac{1}{8}$ in.) around the raw neck edge and machine stitch in place.

Gather the tops of the sleeves, between the notches, and stitch the sleeves to the bodice, adjusting the gathers evenly to fit.

Press under 1 cm ($\frac{3}{8}$ in.), then press under another 2 cm ($\frac{3}{4}$ in.) at the ends of the sleeves. Stitch.

With right sides together, stitch the underarm and bodice side seams.

Gather along the top raw edge of the skirt section, beginning and ending 1 cm ($\frac{3}{8}$ in.) in from the two side edges.

With right sides together, stitch the skirt section to the bodice, adjusting the gathers evenly to fit.

Press under 7 mm ($\frac{1}{4}$ in.) along the bottom raw edge of the coat, and then press under another 3.5 cm ($1\frac{1}{2}$ in.). Stitch. (Before stitching the hem, try the coat on the doll, over a dress, and adjust the hemline if necessary.)

Press under 1 cm ($\frac{3}{8}$ in.) along the front opening edge and stitch, keeping close to the edge.

With the right sides of the two collar pieces together, stitch around the seam allowance, leaving an opening on the inside curved neck edge for turning. Before turning, clip the curves carefully and trim the seam allowance to about 3 mm ($\frac{1}{8}$ in.). Turn the collar right side out. Press, and hand stitch the opening closed. Press again.

Machine stitch around the outside curved edge of the collar, stitching close to the edge.

Pin the collar on to the coat and hand stitch it on.

Sew the two snap fasteners on to the bodice front opening, and decorate by sewing on the four buttons.

Hand sew the lace around the top of the ankle socks.

Hair

Make the hair following the instructions given for Chelsea's hair (*page 42*).

EMBROIDERY

Mouth: use two strands of red, in satin stitch.

Nose: use two strands of black, in a single stitch.

Line around the eye: use two strands of black, in small backstitches.

Eyelashes: use one strand of black, in individual stitches.

Pupil of the eye: use two strands of black, in satin stitch.

Small circle in the eye: use two strands of white, in satin stitch.

Inner area of the iris: use two strands of dark brown, in satin stitch.

Outer area of the iris: use two strands of medium brown, in satin stitch.

Outer area of the eye: use two strands of white, in satin stitch.

Lara

MATERIALS

40 cm (16 in.) of 115 cm (44 in.) wide fabric for the blouse

40 cm (16 in.) of 90 cm (36 in.) wide fabric for the tunic

42 cm (16½ in.) of 3 cm (1¼ in.) wide ribbon and 5 cm (20 in.) of 3 mm (⅛ in.) wide ribbon for the tie, or a strip of striped fabric

25 cm (10 in.) square piece of felt for the beret

5 nylon snap fasteners

3 buttons for the shirt (optional)

embroidery thread for the beret and the shoes

1 packet of One & Only *Wavy Hair*

craft glue

32 cm (13 in.) × 22 cm (9 in.) piece of fabric for the legs

40 cm (16 in.) × 9 cm (3½ in.) piece of fabric for the shoes

PATTERNS

bodice back-no. 28

bodice front-no. 27

collar-no. 45

cuffs – cut two rectangles 16.5 cm (6½ in.) × 6·5 cm (2½ in.)

sleeves-no. 46

tunic top-no. 47

tunic skirt – cut two rectangles 29 cm (11½ in.) × 17 cm (6¾ in.)

tights-no. 6

shoes-no. 11

INSTRUCTIONS

Shirt

With right sides together, stitch the bodice fronts to the bodice back at the shoulders. Press the seams flat. Press under 7 mm (¼ in.) along the front opening edges and machine stitch along them, keeping close to the folded edge.

With the right sides together of the two collar pieces, stitch along three of the sides, leaving the neck edge open. Clip the curves and corners, turn right side out and press. Stitch along the same three sides of the collar, stitching close to the edge.

Tack the collar on to the right side of the shirt, making sure it is in the centre, and leaving a space of approximately 7 mm (¼ in.) at each side.

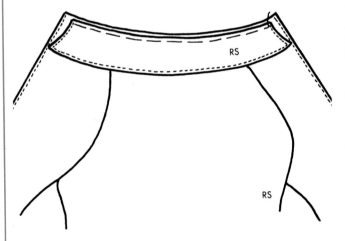

Machine stitch the collar in place.

Fold the raw edge of the collar to the wrong side of the shirt, and machine stitch close to the last row of stitching on the side nearest the raw edge, stitching right out to the front opening edges of the shirt.

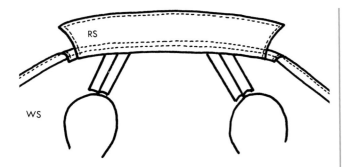

Gather the sleeves between the notches. Pin the sleeves to the bodice, right sides together, matching the notches. Adjust the gathers evenly to fit. Stitch.

Gather the bottom edge of the sleeve to fit one long edge of the cuff. With right sides together, stitch the cuff to the bottom edge of the sleeve. Press under 7 mm ($\frac{1}{4}$ in.) along the other long edge of the cuff. Repeat for the other sleeve.

With right sides together, stitch the underarm and bodice side seams. Fold the cuff in half to the wrong side and hem stitch in place.

At the bottom raw edge of the shirt, press under 7 mm ($\frac{1}{4}$ in.), then press under another 13 mm ($\frac{1}{2}$ in.). Stitch.

Sew on three snap fasteners along the front opening and sew buttons on to the outside.

Tunic

With the right sides together, machine stitch around the two tunic top pieces, leaving them open at the bottom edge. Repeat with the other two pieces. Clip the curves, turn right side out and press.

Mark the centre of each top raw edge of the skirt pieces with a pin. Place another pin 3.5 cm ($1\frac{1}{2}$ in.) on each side of the centre pin. Make a 2·5 cm (1 in.) pleat at these two positions. The overall width of the skirt is now 19 cm ($7\frac{1}{2}$ in.).

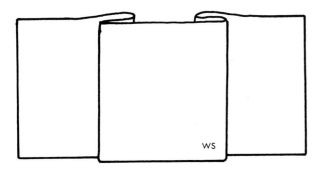

With right sides together, pin the top edge of the skirt to the bottom edge of the tunic top. Note that the skirt section is about 13 mm ($\frac{1}{2}$ in.) wider than the tunic. Leave about 7 mm ($\frac{1}{4}$ in.) on each side of the tunic top. Machine stitch across. Repeat with the other side.

With right sides together, stitch the skirt side seams.

Press under 13 mm ($\frac{1}{2}$ in.) at the hem, then press under another 2.5 cm (1 in.). Machine stitch and press.

With the tunic right side out, oversew the tunic top sides, from the skirt to the armholes.

Sew two snap fasteners at the shoulders.

Tie

If you cannot find striped fabric in the colours you want, make the tie from ribbon, as described here.

Stitch approximately eight diagonal lines of the narrow ribbon across the broad ribbon, evenly spaced.

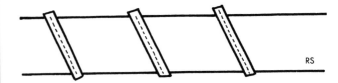

Fold the ribbon in half, with the right sides together.

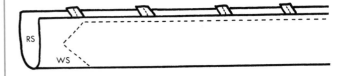

Machine stitch along the long edge, keeping close to the edge and stitching a V-shape at the bottom. Trim away the excess ribbon around the 'V'. Using a thin pencil, turn the tie right side out, and press.

Fold in the raw edges of the ribbon at the open end, and hand stitch the opening closed. Press the tie.

Beret

Cut a circle of felt, 18 cm (7 in.) in diameter.

Put gathering stitches round the edge of the circle, keeping close to the edge. Pull up the gathers until the circle measures 8.5 cm (3¼ in.) in diameter. Secure.

Cut a strip of felt 35 cm (14 in.) × 2 cm (¾ in.). With the right sides of the beret and the strip together, backstitch the strip to the beret. Fold the strip to the inside of the beret and hem in place.

Stitch a tiny, narrow strip of felt to the centre of the beret.

Embroider the badge design on a spare scrap of felt, and hand stitch the badge on to the beret.

Hair

Glue the hair on to the head following the instructions given on the packet.

Shoe laces

Using embroidery thread, stitch an X-shape on the shoe, and tie the ends in a bow.

EMBROIDERY

Mouth: use two strands of red, in small backstitches.

Nose, eyebrows and the line under the eyes: use two strands of light brown, in small backstitches.

Pupil of the eye: use two strands of black, in satin stitch.

Small circle in the eye: use two strands of white, in satin stitch.

Inner area of the iris: use two strands of medium brown, in satin stitch.

Outer area of the iris: use two strands of light brown, in satin stitch.

Eyelashes: use one strand of black, in individual stitches.

James

MATERIALS

40 cm (16 in.) of 115 cm (44 in.) wide fabric for the
shirt

52 cm (21 in.) × 25 cm (10 in.) piece of fabric for the
shorts

42 cm (16½ in.) of 3 cm (1¼ in.) wide ribbon, and
50 cm (20 in.) of 3 mm (⅛ in.) wide ribbon for the
tie, or a strip of striped fabric

two 22 cm (8½ in.) squares of felt for the cap

15 cm (6 in.) of 7 mm (¼ in.) elastic

3 nylon snap fasteners

3 shirt buttons (optional)

embroidery thread for the badge on the cap, and the
shoe laces.

50 g (2 oz) ball of chunky yarn

craft glue

30 cm (12 in.) × 10 cm (4 in.) piece of fabric for the
socks

40 cm (16 in.) × 9 cm (3½ in.) piece of fabric for the
shoes

PATTERNS

bodice back-no. 28

bodice front-no. 27

collar-no. 45

cuffs – cut two rectangles 16.5 cm (6½ in.) × 6.5 cm
(2½ in.)

sleeves-no. 46

shorts-no. 48

pocket-no. 49

cap-no. 50

cap peak-no. 51

knee socks-no. 9

shoes-no. 11

INSTRUCTIONS

Shirt

Follow the instructions given for Lara's school shirt
(*page 52*).

Press under 3 mm (⅛ in.) around the pocket.
Machine stitch around the edge of the pocket.
Position the pocket on the shirt front. Stitch the
pocket to the shirt, leaving the pocket open at the
top.

Tie

Follow the instructions given for Lara's tie (*page 54*).

Shorts

With right sides together, stitch one crotch seam.
(This will become the front seam.)

Press under 7 mm (¼ in.) at the top raw edge of
the shorts, then press under another 2 cm (¾ in.).
Machine stitch. Machine stitch along the top folded
edge, keeping close to the edge.

Attach a 7.5 cm (3 in.) piece of elastic to each side
of the top band, on the wrong side, leaving the
centre 10 cm (4 in.) flat.

At the bottom edge of each leg, press under 7 mm
(¼ in.), then press under another 13 mm (½ in.).
Stitch.

With right sides together, stitch the centre-back
crotch seam. Stitch the inside leg seams. Turn right
side out and press.

Cap

With right sides together, stitch the eight triangular
sections together to form a circle.

Fold under 7 mm ($\frac{1}{4}$ in.) around the bottom and hand stitch in place.

Make a couple of tucks – one on each side of the cap, and stitch in place.

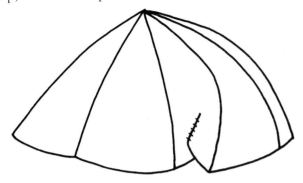

With right sides together, stitch around the outside curved edge of the cap's peak. Trim the seam allowance and turn the peak right side out. Hand stitch it to the front of the cap.

Embroider the badge design on a spare scrap of felt and hand stitch the badge on to the beret.

Hair

Make approximately 22 bunches.

Wrap the yarn around three fingers, eight times. Secure by tying with another piece of yarn. Snip the loops, and glue or stitch the bunches on to the doll's head.

Shoe laces

Using embroidery thread, stitch an X-shape on the shoe and tie the ends into a bow.

EMBROIDERY

Mouth: use two strands of red, in small backstitches.
Nose, the line under the eye and the eyebrows: use two strands of light brown, in small backstitches.
Eyelashes: use one strand of black, in individual stitches.
Pupil of the eye: use two strands of black, in satin stitch.
Inner area of the iris: use medium brown, in satin stitch.
Outer area of the iris: use light brown, in satin stitch.
Small circle in the eye: use two strands of white, in satin stitch.

Lucas

MATERIALS

35 cm (14 in.) of 115 cm (44 in.) wide fabric for the dungarees

30 cm (12 in.) of 115 cm (44 in.) wide fabric for the shirt, patches and pocket

1 m (1 yd) of 7 mm ($\frac{1}{4}$ in.) wide elastic

3 nylon snap fasteners

craft glue

1 packet of One & Only *Curly Hair* (mini-curl)

PATTERNS

bodice back-no. 28
bodice front-no. 27
sleeves-no. 46
neck binding-no. 16
dungaree trousers-no. 29 and no. 52
dungaree bib-no. 31
dungaree shoulder straps-no. 33
dungaree pocket-no. 32
patches-no. 55

INSTRUCTIONS

Shirt

Sew the shirt following the instructions given for Corey's shirt (*page 43*), except for the elastic in the sleeves, which should be sewn on, following the instructions given for the basic dress.

Dungarees

Sew the dungarees, following the instructions given for Sandy's dungarees (*page 27*) until the elastic has been sewn to the top of the legs.

Press under 7 mm ($\frac{1}{4}$ in.) at the bottom raw edge of each leg, then press under another 2 cm ($\frac{3}{4}$ in.). Stitch. Thread a 14 cm ($5\frac{1}{2}$ in.) piece of elastic through this casing, and secure at each end.

Finish the dungarees following the instructions given for Sandy's dungarees (*page 27*).

Press under 7 mm ($\frac{1}{4}$ in.) around the edges of each patch and hand sew the patches onto the dungarees.

Hair

Attach the hair following the instructions on the packet.

59

EMBROIDERY

Mouth: use two strands of red, in small backstitches.

Nose, the line under the eye and the line around the top of the eye: use two strands of black, in small backstitches.

Eyelashes: use one strand of black, in individual stitches.

Pupil of the eye: use two strands of black, in satin stitch.

Small circle in the eye: use two strands of white, in satin stitch.

Iris of the eye: use two strands of light brown, in satin stitch.

Outer area of the eye: use two strands of white, in satin stitch.

Glasses: use two strands of pale grey, in small backstitches.

Libby

MATERIALS

60 cm (24 in.) of 115 cm (44 in.) wide fabric for the dress

30 cm (12 in.) of 115 cm (44 in.) wide fabric for the apron

fabric scraps for rag ribbons (optional)

25 cm (10 in.) of 7 mm ($\frac{1}{4}$ in.) wide elastic

3 nylon snap fasteners

50 g (2 oz) ball of mohair yarn

craft glue

PATTERNS

bodice front-no. 14

bodice back-no. 15

sleeves-no. 13

neck binding-no. 16

skirt – cut one rectangle 110 cm (44 in.) × 25 cm (10 in.). See pattern no. 24 for markings

apron skirt – cut one rectangle 53 cm (21 in.) × 20 cm (8 in.).

apron waist band-no. 56

apron bib – cut one rectangle 6.5 cm ($2\frac{1}{2}$ in.) × 11.5 cm ($4\frac{1}{2}$ in.)

apron frill – cut two strips 24 cm ($9\frac{1}{2}$ in.) × 3.5 cm ($1\frac{1}{2}$ in.)

apron straps-no. 57

INSTRUCTIONS

Dress

Sew the dress following the instructions given for the basic dress.

Apron

Press under 7 mm ($\frac{1}{4}$ in.) at the side edges of the apron skirt, then press under another 13 mm ($\frac{1}{2}$ in.). Stitch in place.

Press under 7 mm ($\frac{1}{4}$ in.), then press under another 2 cm ($\frac{3}{4}$ in.) at the bottom edge of the apron skirt. Stitch.

Gather across the top edge of the apron and, with right sides together, pin it to the waist band between the dots. Adjust the gathers evenly and stitch.

Press the seam allowance towards the waistband, continuing to press up to the ends of the waist band.

Press under 7 mm ($\frac{1}{4}$ in.) along the other long edge of the waist band.

Fold the waist band in half lengthways, with right sides together. Stitch the ends and clip the corners.

Turn the waist band right side out and stitch all the way round, keeping close to the edge.

Press under 3 mm ($\frac{1}{8}$ in.) along one long edge of each frill, then press under another 3 mm ($\frac{1}{8}$ in.). Stitch in place.

Gather along the other long edge.

With right sides together, pin the frill to one long edge of the shoulder strap, adjusting gathers to fit. Stitch in place.

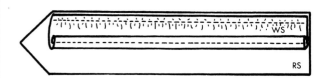

Repeat with the other frill and strap, reversing the side of the strap on to which the frill is sewn.

Press under 7 mm ($\frac{1}{4}$ in.) along the other long edge of the shoulder strap. Fold it in half lengthways

with right sides out. Press. Stitch in place, keeping close to the edge.

Press the bib in half, widthways, with the right sides out.

Stitch the straps to the bib, overlapping the bib by 7 mm ($\frac{1}{4}$ in.).

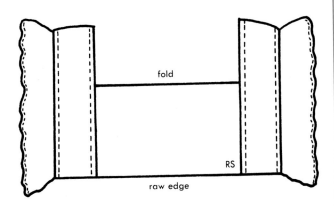

Stitch the bib section to the centre front of the apron, overlapping the bib and the waist band by 7 mm ($\frac{1}{4}$ in.).

Tie the apron around the doll and pin the straps into position at the back. Stitch the straps to the waist band.

Hair

Make approximately 20 bunches.

Wrap the yarn around four fingers, eight times, and secure by tying tightly with another piece of the yarn.

Glue or stitch the bunches on to the head.

If you have any scraps of fabric, you can use them to make rag ribbons. Cut your fabric into strips and tie a knot in each strip. Then, glue or stitch the rag ribbons on to the head.

EMBROIDERY

Mouth: use two strands of red, in small backstitches.
Nose, eyebrows, the line under the eyes and the line around the top of the eyes: use two strands of black, in small backstitches.
Eyelashes: use one strand of black, in small backstitches.
Pupil of the eye: use two strands of black, in satin stitch.
Small circle in the eye: use two strands of white, in satin stitch.
Iris: use two strands of light brown, in satin stitch.
Outer area of the eye: use two strands of white, in satin stitch.

Fleur

MATERIALS

80 cm (32 in.) of 115 cm (44 in.) wide fabric for the dress

50 cm (20 in.) of 4 cm ($1\frac{3}{4}$ in.) wide lace with ribbon inset

1 m (1 yd) of 3.5 cm ($1\frac{1}{2}$ in.) wide pre-gathered lace, with a scalloped edge

1.25 m ($1\frac{1}{4}$ yd) of 7 mm ($\frac{1}{4}$ in.) ribbon

12 ribbon roses in three different colours

3 nylon snap fasteners

50 g (2 oz) ball of mohair yarn

craft glue

PATTERNS

bodice front-no. 14

bodice back-no. 15

sleeves-no. 58

neck binding-no. 16

skirt – cut two rectangles, one 110 cm (44 in.) × 25 cm (10 in.), the other 110 cm (44 in.) × 22.5 cm (9 in.)

INSTRUCTIONS

Dress

Stitch the shoulder seams, sew on the lace and neck binding and attach the sleeves following the instructions given for Willow's dress (*page 21*).

Sew a 25 cm (10 in.) piece of lace to the bottom edge of each of the sleeves, following the instructions given for attaching the lace to Chelsea's petticoat (*page 40*).

Attach a 13 cm (5 in.) piece of elastic 1.5 cm ($\frac{5}{8}$ in.) in from the finished fabric edge of the sleeve.

With right sides together, stitch the underarm and bodice side seams.

Tack the two skirt pieces together, with the shortest on top, stitching along the top raw edge 13 mm ($\frac{1}{2}$ in.) down from the top, and stopping 2 cm ($\frac{3}{4}$ in.) in from each side edge.

Gather across the top in three sections, starting and stopping 2 cm ($\frac{3}{4}$ in.) in from each of the edges:

First gather for 26.5 cm ($10\frac{1}{2}$ in.).

Secondly, gather for 53 cm ($21\frac{1}{2}$ in.).

Thirdly, gather for 26.5 cm ($10\frac{1}{2}$ in.).

Do not pull the gathers up yet.

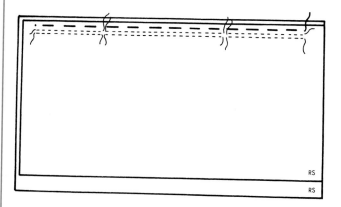

With right sides together, fold the skirt in half lengthways. Stitch each of the two skirt back seams, starting at the bottom and stopping 4.5 cm ($1\frac{3}{4}$ in.) from the top raw edge.

Press under 7 mm ($\frac{1}{4}$ in.) at the bottom of each skirt hem, and press under another 2.5 cm (1 in.). Stitch.

Attach the skirt to the bodice following the instructions given for the basic dress.

Press under 7 mm ($\frac{1}{4}$ in.) along the back opening edges, and stitch from the neck to the bottom of the bodice, keeping close to the edge.

Sew on the snap fasteners.

Using small running stitches, gather up four lines, each 7 cm (2¾ in.) long, evenly spaced around the bottom edge of the top skirt. Pull up the gathers and secure.

Cut four 13 cm (5 in.) pieces of 3.5 cm (1½ in.) wide scalloped lace.

With small running stitches, gather up the straight edges of the lace to form a circle. Stitch the two raw edges together.

Stitch the lace circles to the four gathered areas of the dress. Make four bows with ribbon and stitch these on to the circles of lace.

Hand stitch on three ribbon roses.

Hair

Make approximately 20 bunches.

Wrap the yarn around three fingers, eight times, and secure by tying tightly with another piece of the yarn.

Glue or stitch the bunches on to the head.

Make three bows from the ribbon, and glue or stitch them on to the head.

EMBROIDERY

Mouth: use two strands of pink, in small backstitches.

Freckles: use two strands of light brown, in individual stitches.

Nose, eyelids and eyebrows: use two strands of light brown, in small backstitches.

Eyelashes: use one strand of black, in individual long stitches.

Pupil of the eye: use two strands of black, in satin stitch.

Inner area of the iris: use two strands of dark brown, in satin stitch.

Outer area of the iris: use two strands of light brown, in satin stitch.

Small circle in the eye: use two strands of white, in satin stitch.

Megan

MATERIALS

40 cm (16 in.) of 115 cm (44 in.) wide fabric for the
  blouse and the waist band
35 cm (14 in.) of 115 cm (44 in) wide fabric for the
  pinafore
110 cm (44 in.) of 2.5 cm (1 in.) wide lace
25 cm (10 in) of 7 mm ($\frac{1}{4}$ in.) elastic
60 cm (24 in.) of narrow ribbon
5 nylon snap fasteners
50 g (2 oz) ball of mohair yarn
craft glue

PATTERNS

bodice back-no. 37
bodice front-no. 38
sleeves-no. 13
neck binding-no. 16
pinafore bib-no. 59
waist band – cut two rectangles 58 cm (23 in.) ×
  7.5 cm (3 in.)
skirt – cut two rectangles 55 cm (22 in.) × 18 cm
  (7 in.)

INSTRUCTIONS

Blouse

Stitch the shoulder seams, sew on the neck binding
and attach the sleeves, following the instructions
given for the basic dress. Note that the bodice front
of the basic dress is the bodice back of the blouse.

Press under 7 mm ($\frac{1}{4}$ in.) along the bottom raw
edge of the blouse, then press under another 13 mm
($\frac{1}{2}$ in.) and stitch.

Sew three snap fasteners on to the front opening.

Pinafore

Sew a 55 cm (22 in.) long piece of lace to the bottom
edge of each skirt piece, following the instructions
given for attaching the lace to Chelsea's petticoat
(*page 40*).

Gather along the top raw edge of each skirt piece,
starting and stopping 13 mm ($\frac{1}{2}$ in.) in from the side
edges.

With the right sides together of the two pinafore
bib pieces, machine stitch around them, leaving them
open at the bottom edge. Repeat with the other two
pieces. Clip the curves, turn them right side out and
then press.

To make the waist bands, fold the strips in half
lengthways, with the right sides together, and stitch
along one short edge and one long edge, leaving it
open at the other short edge for turning. Repeat for
the other waist band. Turn them right side out and
fold in the open edge 7 mm ($\frac{1}{4}$ in.). Hand stitch the
opening closed. Press.

Match the centre of each waist band to the centre
of each bib. Set the folded edge of the waist band
over the bib, overlapping by 7 mm ($\frac{1}{4}$ in.). Stitch the
waist band to the bib, keeping close to the folded
edge of the waist band.

With right sides together of the two skirt pieces,
stitch the side seams, stopping 5 cm (2 in.) from the
top raw edge. Press the seam flat and continue
pressing up to the top raw edge.

Pull up the gathers and sew the skirt to the lower
edge of the waist band, overlapping by 7 mm ($\frac{1}{4}$ in.)
and coming out 2.5 cm (1 in.) wider than the bib
section. Stitch close to the lower edge of the waist
band.

Sew two snap fasteners on to the shoulders of the
bib.

Hair

Using a piece of cardboard 18 cm (7 in.) long by at least 10 cm (4 in.) wide, follow the instructions given for Hannah's hair (*page 18*) (making the mat of yarn 10 cm (4 in.) wide), as far as having torn off the tissue paper.

Using another piece of card 3.5 cm (1½ in.) long by at least 5 cm (2 in.) wide, make the fringe in the same way.

Glue or stitch the fringe on to the top of the head. Glue or stitch the main piece of the hair on with the seam running from the front to the back, overlapping the fringe.

Tie up into bunches using another piece of the yarn. Finally, tie on some ribbon.

EMBROIDERY

Mouth: use two strands of pink, in satin stitch for the circles, and in small backstitches for the line.
Nose: use two strands of medium brown, in small backstitches.
Eyebrows and the line around the outside of the eyes: use two strands of dark brown, in small backstitches.
Eyelashes: use one strand of dark brown, in small backstitches.
Pupil of the eye: use two strands of black, in satin stitch.

Small circle in the eye: use two strands of white, in satin stitch for each eye.
Inner area of the iris: use two strands of dark brown, in satin stitch.
Outer area of the iris: use two strands of medium brown, in satin stitch.

Santa Claus

MATERIALS

30 cm (12 in.) of 115 cm (44 in.) wide fabric for the shirt

60 cm (24 in.) of 115 cm (44 in.) wide fabric for the suit

40 cm (16 in.) × 20 cm (8 in.) piece of fabric for the boots

15 cm (6 in.) of 115 cm (44 in.) wide fur fabric

3 nylon snap fasteners

45 cm (18 in.) of 7 mm ($\frac{1}{4}$ in.) wide elastic

1 packet of One & Only *Curly Hair* (maxi-curl)

1 large brass bell

49 cm (19 in.) × 4 cm ($1\frac{3}{4}$ in.) piece of fabric for the belt

PATTERNS

jacket back-no. 64

jacket front-no. 65

jacket sleeves – cut two rectangles 20 cm (8 in.) × 13 cm (5 in.)

trousers-no. 29 and no. 66

straps-no. 33

hat-no. 67

shirt bodice back-no. 37

shirt bodice front-no. 38

shirt sleeves-no. 46

neck binding-no. 16

legs no. 8

boots-no. 10

nose-no. 68

INSTRUCTIONS

Jacket

With right sides together, stitch the bodice fronts to the bodice back at the shoulders. Press the seams flat.

Press under 7 mm ($\frac{1}{4}$ in.) around the neck edge and stitch, keeping close to the edge.

Fold the sleeve in half lengthways to find the centre of the top edge. With the right sides together, and placing the centre mark over the shoulder seam, stitch the sleeve to the jacket.

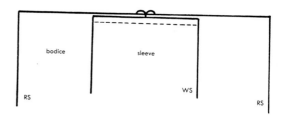

With the right sides of the coat together, stitch the underarm seams.

Stitch the jacket side seams.

Press or fold under 13 mm ($\frac{1}{2}$ in.) at the end of the sleeve and stitch, keeping close to the edge.

Press or fold under 7 mm ($\frac{1}{4}$ in) along the bottom edge and stitch, keeping close to the edge.

Cut strips of fur fabric 3.5 cm ($1\frac{1}{2}$ in.) wide, and hand stitch them around the neck edge, bottom edge, one front opening edge and around the bottom of the sleeves.

Fold or press under 7 mm ($\frac{1}{4}$ in.) along the two long edges of the belt fabric. Hand stitch the belt around the jacket, folding under the raw edges at the ends.

Trousers

Sew the trousers following the instructions given for Corey's trousers (*page 43*). Before stitching the inside leg seams, press or fold under 13 mm ($\frac{1}{2}$ in.) along the bottom edges of each trouser leg and stitch, keeping close to the edge.

Cut two strips of fur fabric 3.5 cm ($1\frac{1}{2}$ in.) wide, and hand stitch them to the bottom edges of each trouser leg.

Hat

Fold the hat in half lengthways and machine stitch along the curved edge. Trim the seam allowance at the pointed tip of the hat. Turn the hat right side out.

Press or fold under 7 mm ($\frac{1}{4}$ in.) at the bottom edge of the hat and stitch, keeping close to the edge.

Cut a strip of fur fabric 3.5 cm ($1\frac{1}{2}$ in.) wide and sew it on to the hat.

Sew the bell on to the point of the hat.

Shirt

Sew the shirt, following the instructions given for Corey's shirt (*page 43*).

Nose

Sew on the nose, following the instructions given on *page 13*.

Hair and beard

Glue or stitch the hair on, following the instructions given on the packet.

Sew the hat on to Santa's head.

EMBROIDERY

Mouth: use two strands of red, in satin stitch.

Line under the eye and around the top of the eye: use two strands of dark brown, in small backstitches.

Pupil of the eye: use two strands of black, in satin stitch.

Small circle in the eye: use two strands of white, in satin stitch.

Inner area of the iris: use two strands of dark brown, in satin stitch.

Outer area of the iris: use two strands of medium brown, in satin stitch.

Eyelashes: use one strand of black, in individual stitches.

Mrs Claus

MATERIALS

65 cm (26 in.) of 115 cm (44 in.) wide fabric for the
    dress and the patches on the apron

35 cm (14 in.) of 90 cm (36 in.) wide fabric for the
    apron

25 cm (10 in.) of 7 mm ($\frac{1}{4}$ in.) wide elastic

23 cm (9 in.) of 35 mm ($1\frac{1}{2}$ in.) wide pre-gathered lace

3 nylon snap fasteners

half a packet of One & Only *Curly Hair* (maxi-curl)

craft glue

60 cm (24 in.) of narrow ribbon

PATTERNS

bodice front-no. 14

bodice back-no. 15

sleeves-no. 13

neck binding-no. 16

skirt – cut one rectangle 110 cm (44 in.) × 29 cm
    (11$\frac{1}{2}$ in.) See pattern no. 24 for the markings along
    the top edge, noting that the example shown is
    shorter in length

apron skirt – cut one rectangle 32 cm (12$\frac{3}{4}$ in.) ×
    30 cm (12 in.) wide

apron waist band-no. 25

heart patches-no. 69

bun-no. 70

nose-no. 68

INSTRUCTIONS

Dress

Sew the dress, following the instructions given for
Willow's dress (*page 21*).

Apron

Cut out the heart shapes using paper. Pin the paper
on to the fabric and cut around the shape, adding on
about 7 mm ($\frac{1}{4}$ in.) all round as you cut.

    Press the fabric over the paper and pin the extra
fabric to the wrong side. Press again. Remove the
paper and press again.

    Position the hearts on the apron and hand stitch
them in place.

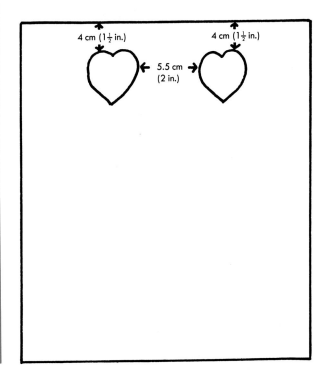

Press under 7 mm ($\frac{1}{4}$ in.) along the top edge of the pocket and stitch, keeping close to the edge.

Make a fold in the apron as shown and press.

Stitch a line down the centre of the pocket.

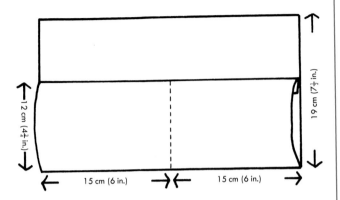

Press under 7 mm ($\frac{1}{4}$ in.) at each side edge and press under another 7 mm ($\frac{1}{4}$ in.). Stitch.

Gather along the top edge of the apron and finish, following the instructions given for Willow's apron (*page 21*).

Bun

Sew a line of running stitches around the bun, about 7 mm ($\frac{1}{4}$ in.) in from the edge. Gather up until the opening is about 3.5 cm ($1\frac{1}{2}$ in.) wide. Secure the gathering thread.

Stuff the bun and sew it on top of Mrs Claus's head, slightly towards the back.

Glue on the hair, following the instructions given on the packet.

Tie the ribbon around the base of the bun.

Nose

Sew on the nose, following the instructions given on *page 13*.

EMBROIDERY

Mouth: use two strands of red, in small backstitches.

Line under the eye and around the top of the eye: use two strands of dark brown, in small backstitches.

Eyebrows: use two strands of white, in small backstitches.

Eyelashes: use one strand of brown, in individual stitches.

Pupil of the eye: use two strands of black, in satin stitch.

Small circle in the eye: use two strands of white, in satin stitch.

Inner area of the iris: use two strands of dark brown, in satin stitch.

Outer area of the iris: use two strands of medium brown, in satin stitch.

Elf

MATERIALS

50 cm (20 in.) of 115 cm (44 in.) wide fabric for the
tunic

30 cm (12 in.) of 115 cm (44 in.) wide fabric for the
legs and the scarf

one 23 cm (9 in.) square piece of felt for the shoes

one 34 cm (13 in.) × 20 cm (8 in.) piece of felt for
the hat

scrap of the body fabric for the ears and nose

4 nylon snap fasteners

2 small brass bells and 1 large brass bell

1 packet of One & Only *Curly Hair* (maxi-curl)

craft glue

PATTERNS

tunic bodice front-no. 71

tunic bodice back-no. 72

sleeves – cut two rectangles 19 cm (7½ in.) × 6 cm
(2½ in.)

zigzag trim-no. 73

shoes-no. 74

ears-no. 17

nose-no. 68

scarf-no. 75

hat-no. 67

INSTRUCTIONS

Tunic

With right sides together, stitch the bodice backs to
the bodice front at the shoulders.

Press the seams flat.

Sew on the sleeves following the instructions
given for Santa's jacket (*page 71*).

Press under 7 mm (¼ in.) at the bottom edge of the
sleeves and stitch, keeping close to the edge.

Press under 3 mm (⅛ in.) around the neck edge of
the tunic and stitch, keeping close to the edge.

Press under 13 mm (½ in.) along both back
opening edges and stitch, keeping close to the edge.

With the right sides of the zigzag trim together,
machine stitch up and down along the zigzag edge
of the trim, leaving it open at the top.

Carefully trim the seam allowance at the points
and turn it right side out. Press.

Gather along the top open edge of the trim and,
with right sides together, pin the trim to the bodice,
gathering slightly to fit. Stitch the trim to the
bodice.

Sew on three snap fasteners at the back opening.

Shoes

Make two.

Fold over 1 cm (⅜ in.) along the top long edge of
the felt and pin to secure. Fold this strip in half.

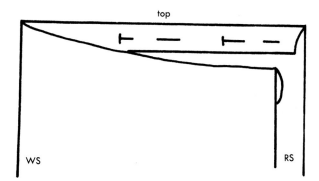

Place the shoe pattern on top of the felt and draw
around it. Stitch along this line.

Trim along the seam allowance, especially at the

curl, to 3 mm ($\frac{1}{8}$ in.) or less. Turn right side out.

Sew a small brass bell on to the tip of the curl.

Hat

Stitch along the curved edge of the hat. Trim the seam allowance and turn the hat right side out.

Fold up 2.5 cm (1 in.) along the bottom edge. Sew a large brass bell on to the point of the hat.

Scarf

With right sides together, stitch all around the scarf, leaving open between the dots.

Clip the corners and turn the scarf right side out. Press.

Hand stitch the opening closed. Sew a snap fastener on to the front.

Nose

Follow the instructions given on *page 13.*

Ears

With the right sides together of two ear pieces, stitch around the outside curved edge.

Clip the seam allowance and turn right side out. Insert a small piece of stuffing and spread it out evenly.

Fold inside 7 mm ($\frac{1}{4}$ in.) at the open edge of the ear and hand stitch it closed.

With small running stitches, stitch a line along the outside curved edge of the ear, 3 mm ($\frac{1}{8}$ in.) in from the edge.

Hand stitch the ears on to the head.

Hair

Sew or glue on the hair following the instructions on the packet.

EMBROIDERY

Mouth: use two strands of red, in small backstitches.

Eyebrows and around the outer circle of the eyes: Use two strands of dark brown, in small backstitches.

Eyelashes: use one strand of black, in individual long stitches.

Centre circle of the eyes: use two strands of black, in satin stitch.

Outer circle of the eyes: use two strands of dark brown, in satin stitch.

Suppliers

The materials to make the dolls are readily available at most fabric and wool shops, with the exception of the polypropylene hair. This is made in the USA by a company called 'One & Only creations' and is available from craft shops in Great Britain, the USA and Canada. The company's address is:

One & Only Creations
P.O. Box 2730
Napa
CA 94558
USA

The hair is also available by mail order from two addresses in Great Britain:

Dainty Toys
Unit 35
Phoenix Road
Crowther Industrial Estate
District 3
Washington
Tyne and Wear
NE38 0AB
Tel: (091) 4167886/4176277

Panduro Hobby
Westway House
Transport Avenue
Brentford
Middlesex
TW8 9HF
Tel: (081) 847 6161

The fabrics for the dolls' clothes are also available by mail order:

Village Fabrics Retail
P.O. Box 43
Wallingford
Oxon
OX10 9DF
Tel: (0491) 836178

Calico Threads
57 Marine Parade
Dunoon
Argyll
PA23 8HF
Tel: (0369) 3007

Patterns

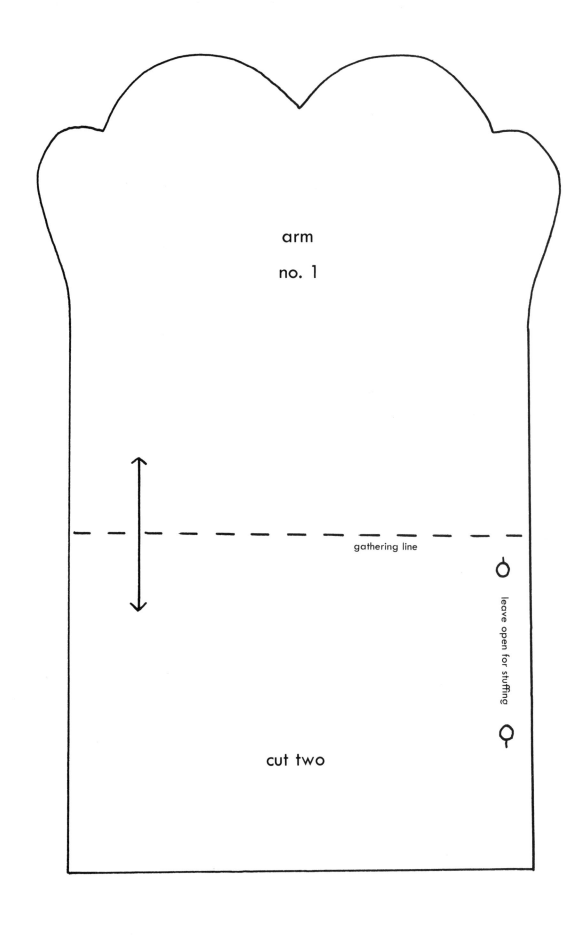

arm

no. 1

gathering line

leave open for stuffing

cut two

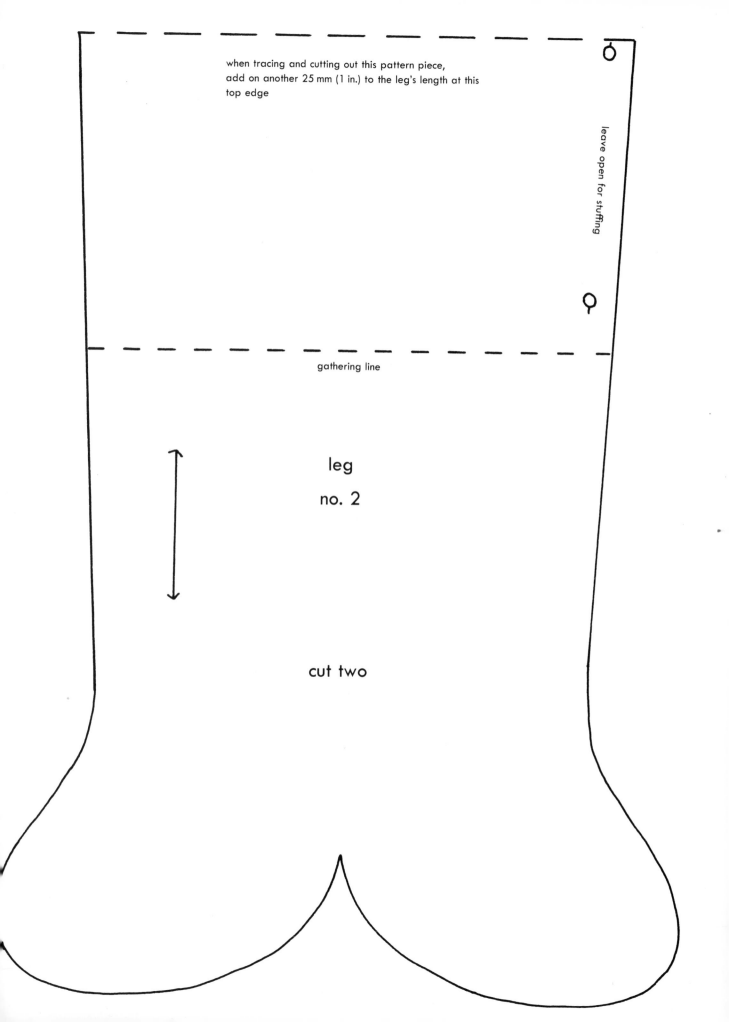

when tracing and cutting out this pattern piece,
add on another 25 mm (1 in.) to the leg's length at this
top edge

leave open for stuffing

gathering line

leg

no. 2

cut two

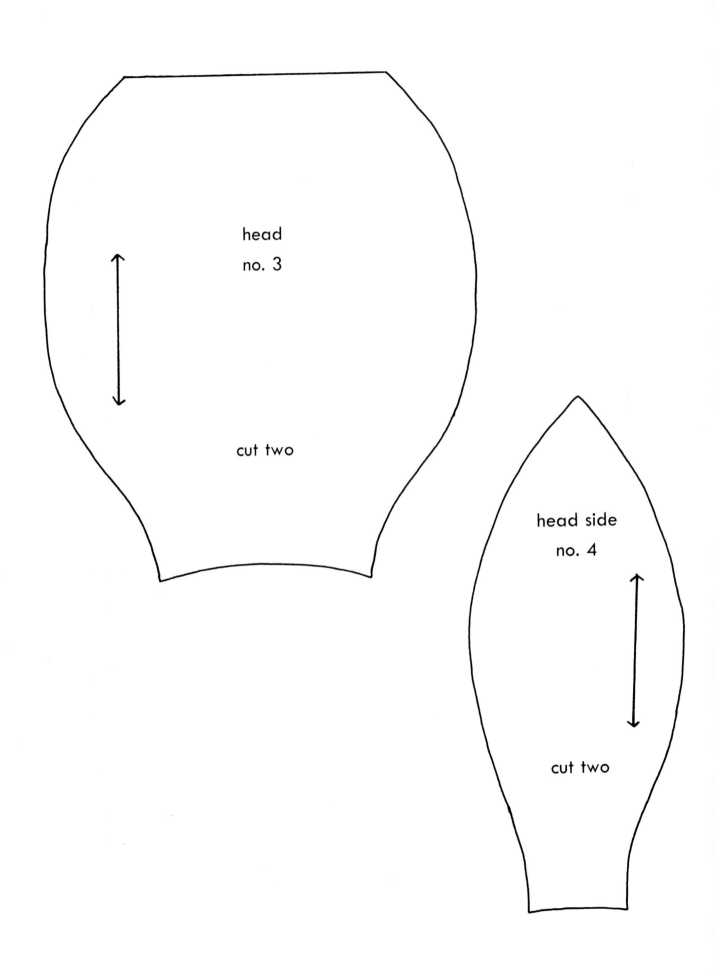

head

no. 3

cut two

head side

no. 4

cut two

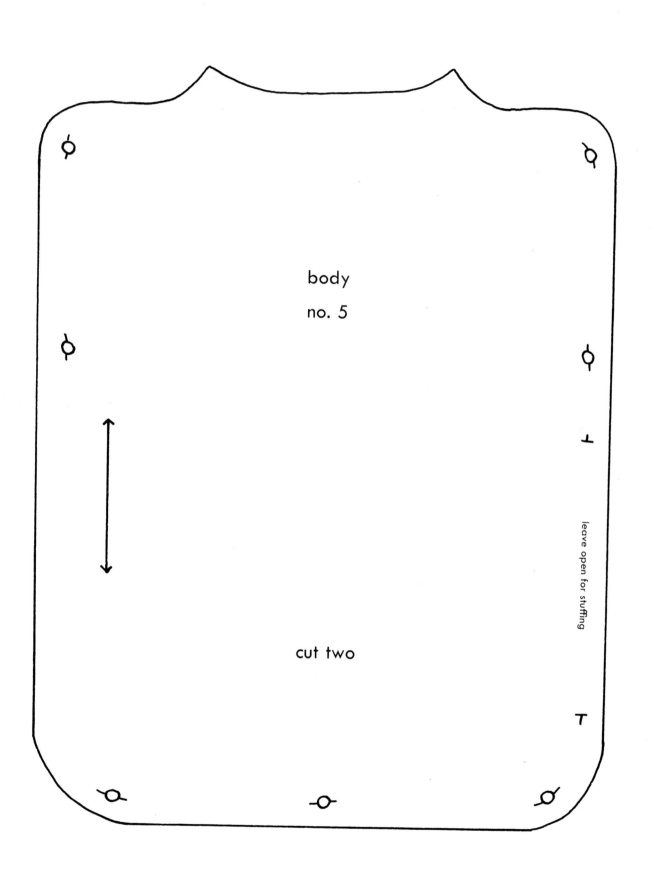

body

no. 5

leave open for stuffing

cut two

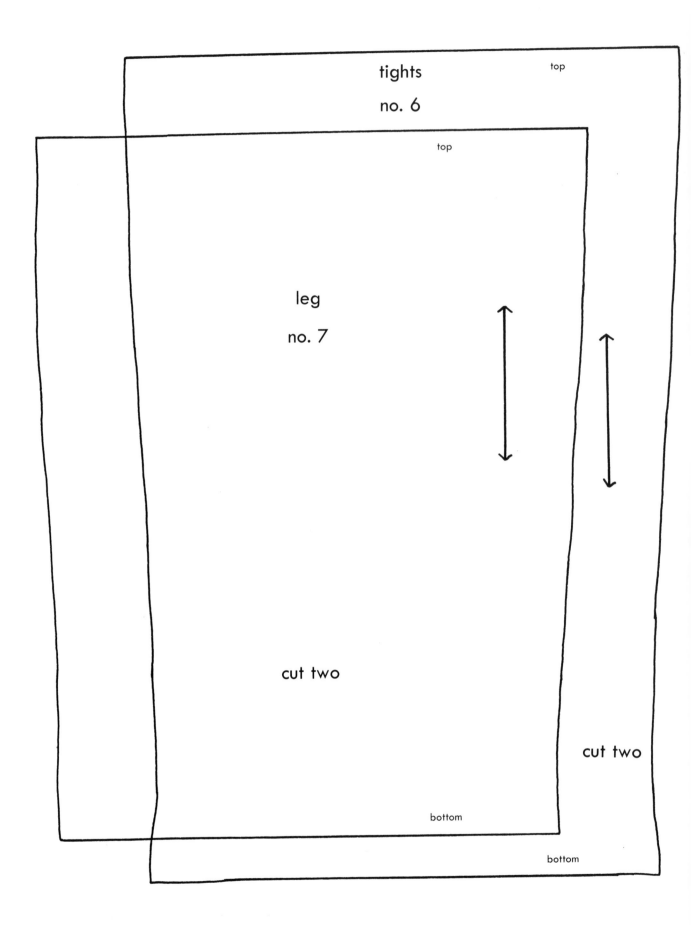

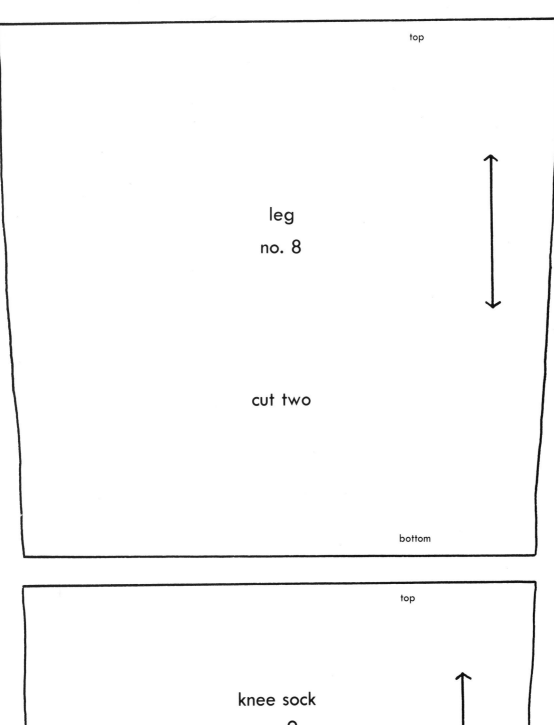

top

leg

no. 8

cut two

bottom

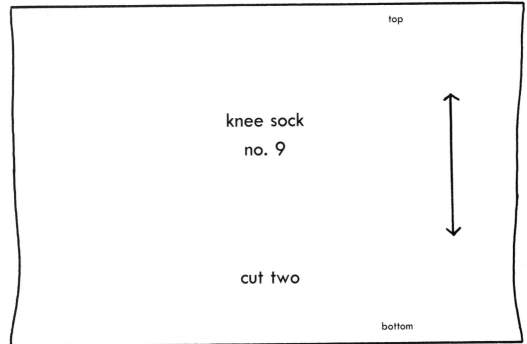

top

knee sock

no. 9

cut two

bottom

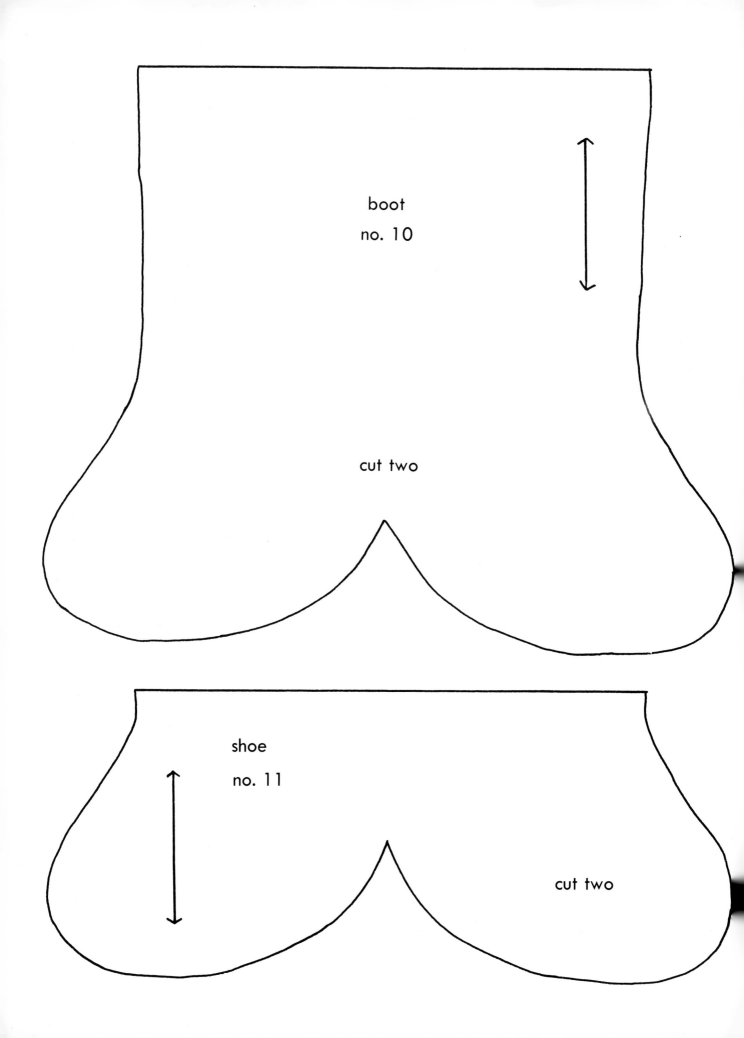

boot
no. 10

cut two

shoe

no. 11

cut two

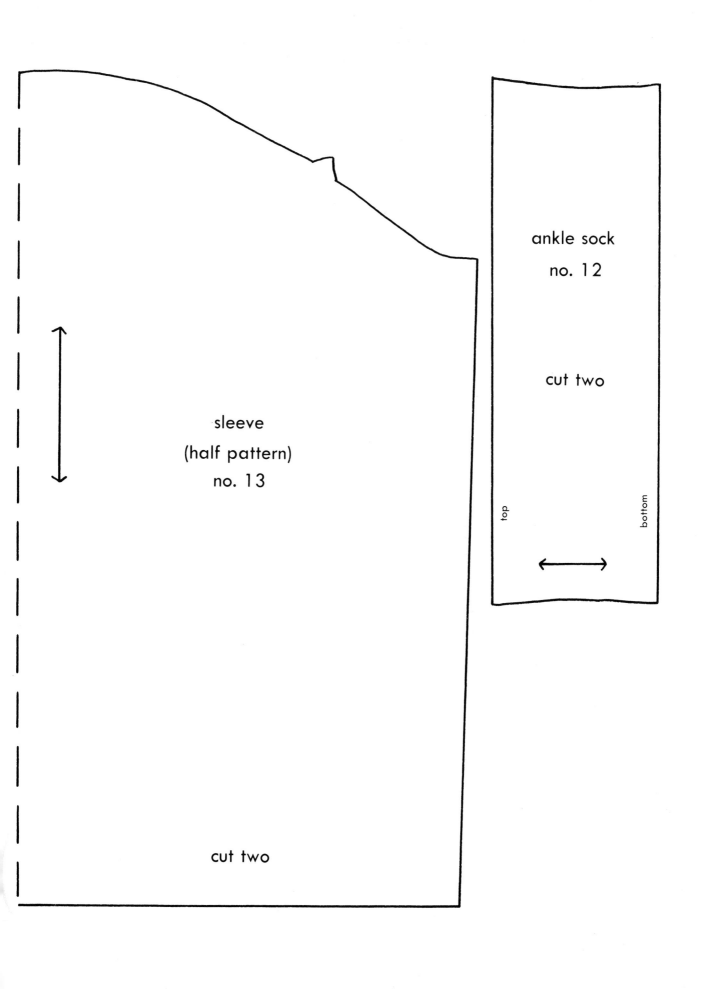

ankle sock
no. 12

cut two

top

bottom

sleeve
(half pattern)
no. 13

cut two

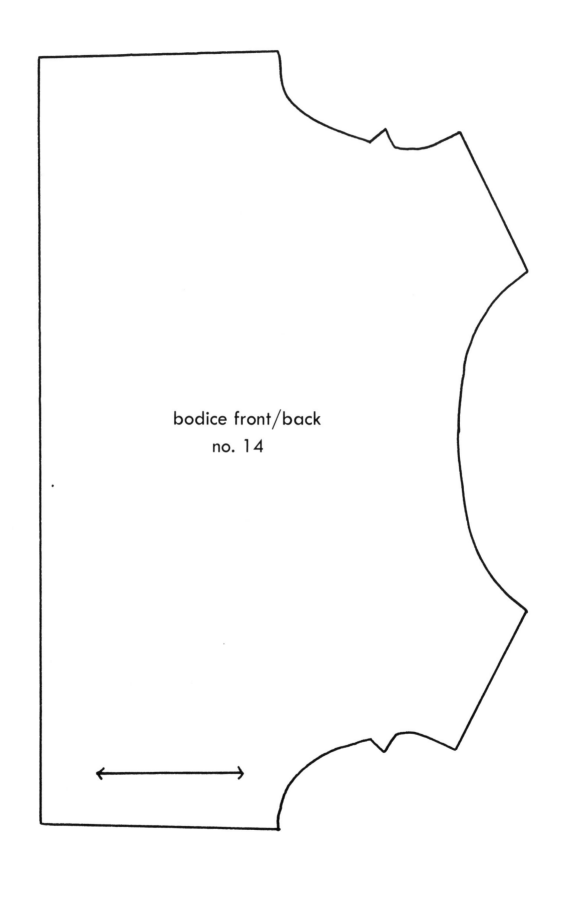

bodice front/back
no. 14

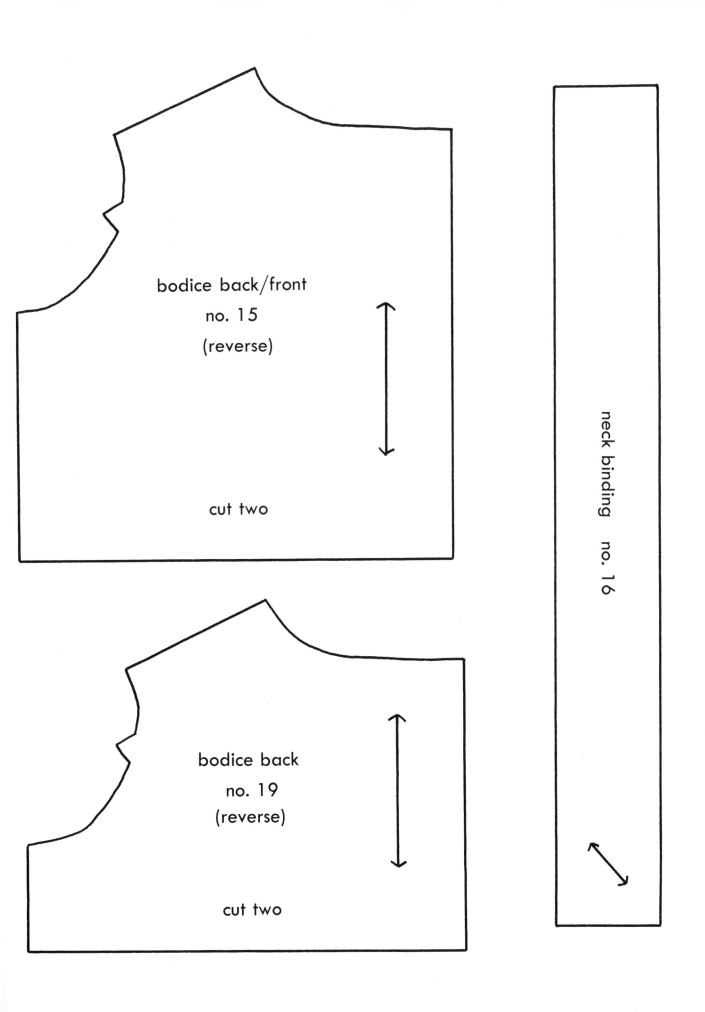

bodice back/front

no. 15

(reverse)

cut two

bodice back

no. 19

(reverse)

cut two

neck binding   no. 16

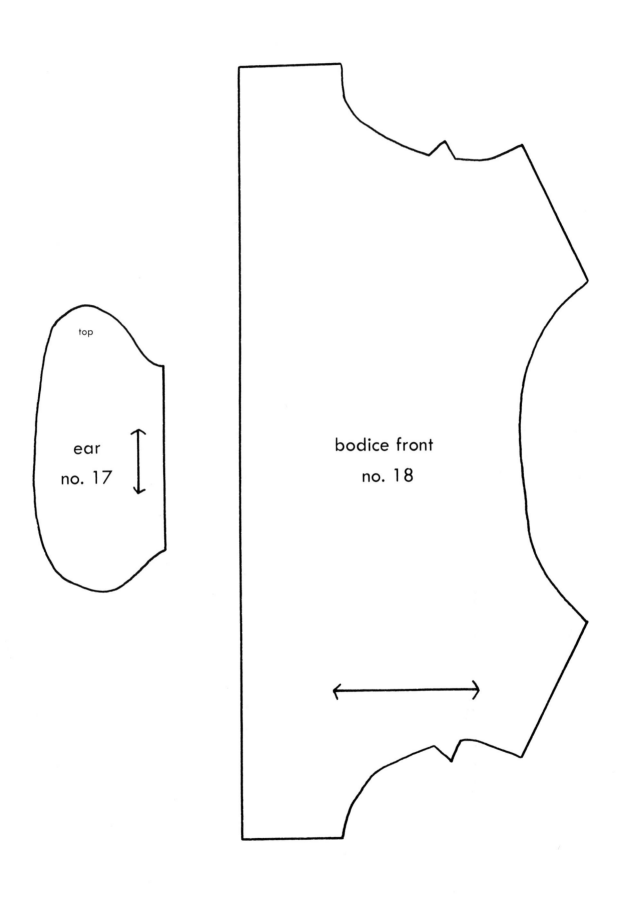

top

ear
no. 17

bodice front
no. 18

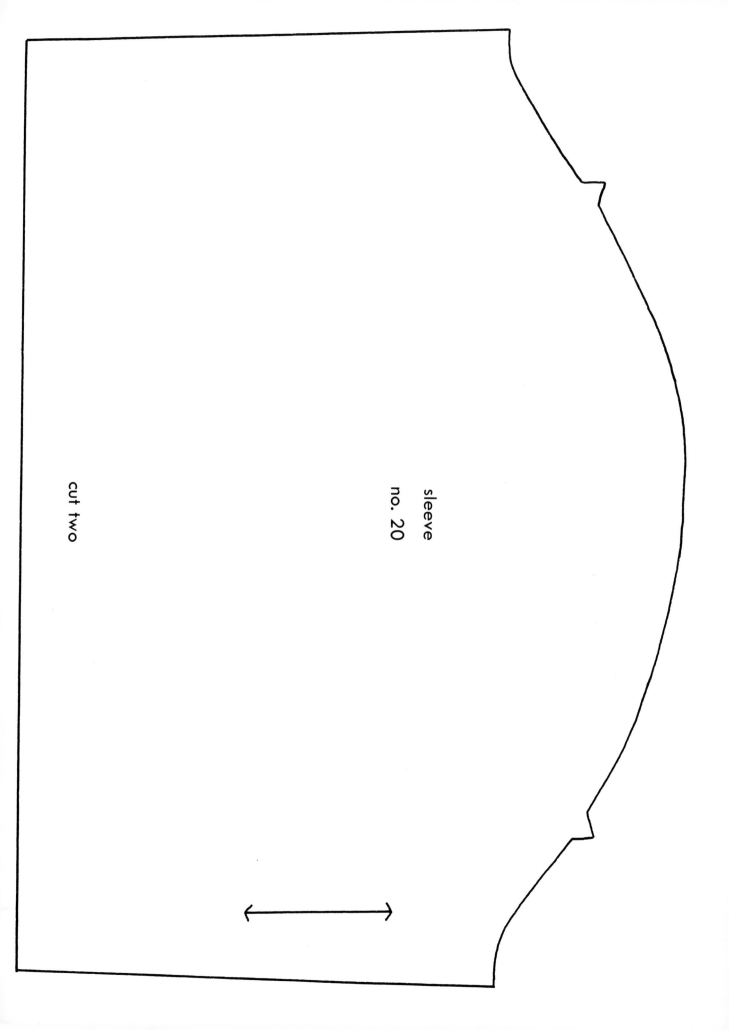

sleeve

no. 20

cut two

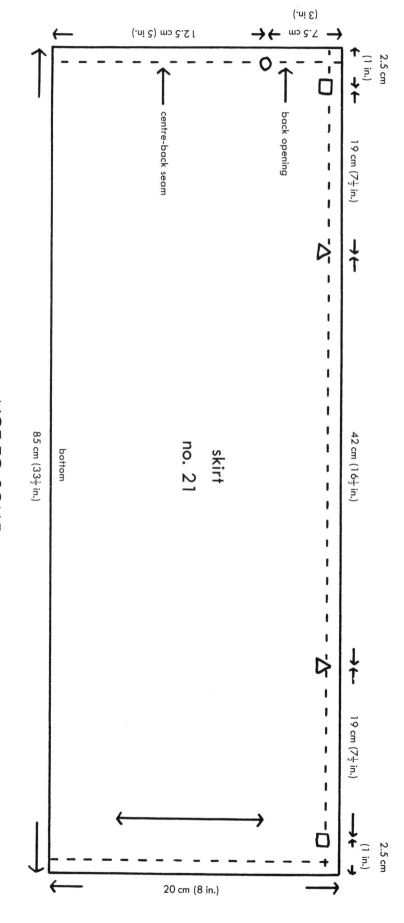

NOT TO SCALE

skirt
no. 21

bottom

centre-back seam

back opening

2.5 cm
(1 in.)

7.5 cm
(3 in.)

12.5 cm (5 in.)

19 cm (7½ in.)

42 cm (16½ in.)

19 cm (7½ in.)

2.5 cm
(1 in.)

85 cm (33½ in.)

20 cm (8 in.)

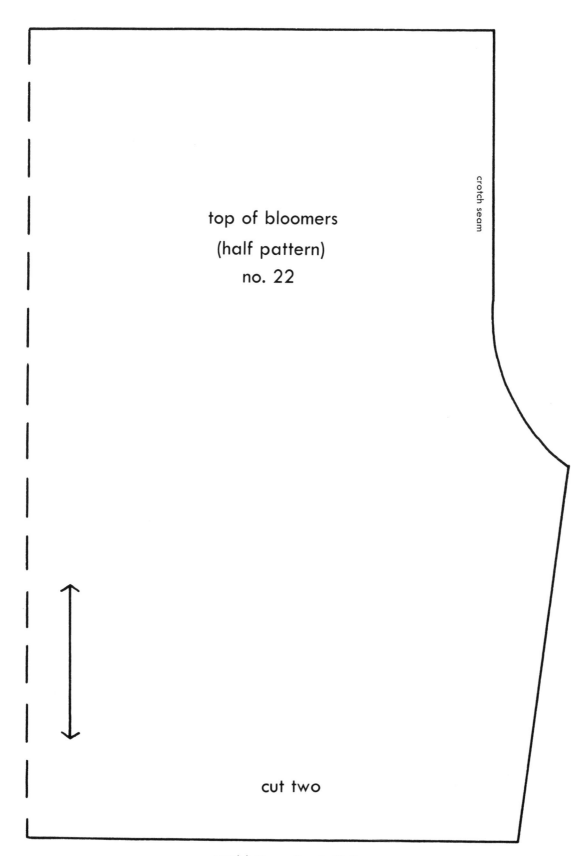

top of bloomers
(half pattern)
no. 22

crotch seam

cut two

match bottom pattern to this line

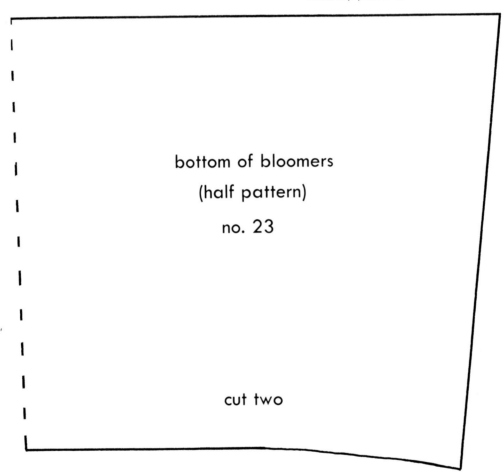

bottom of bloomers
(half pattern)
no. 23

cut two

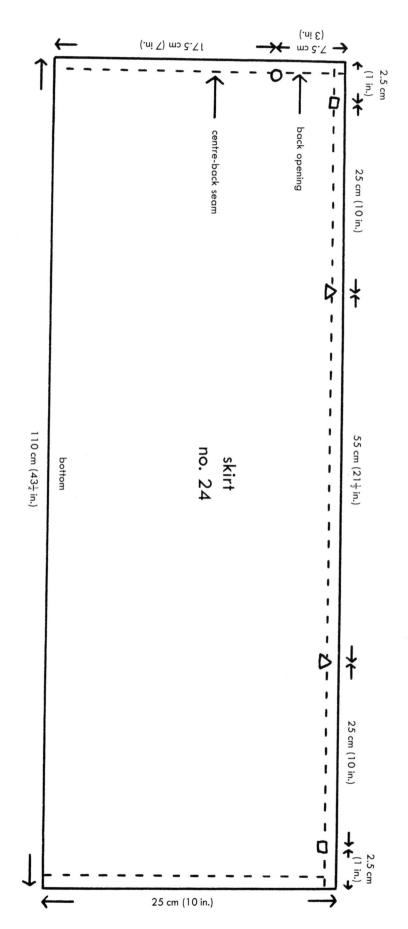

NOT TO SCALE

110 cm (43¼ in.)

bottom

skirt
no. 24

centre-back seam

back opening

2.5 cm
(1 in.)

17.5 cm (7 in.)

7.5 cm
(3 in.)

25 cm (10 in.)

55 cm (21½ in.)

25 cm (10 in.)

2.5 cm
(1 in.)

25 cm (10 in.)

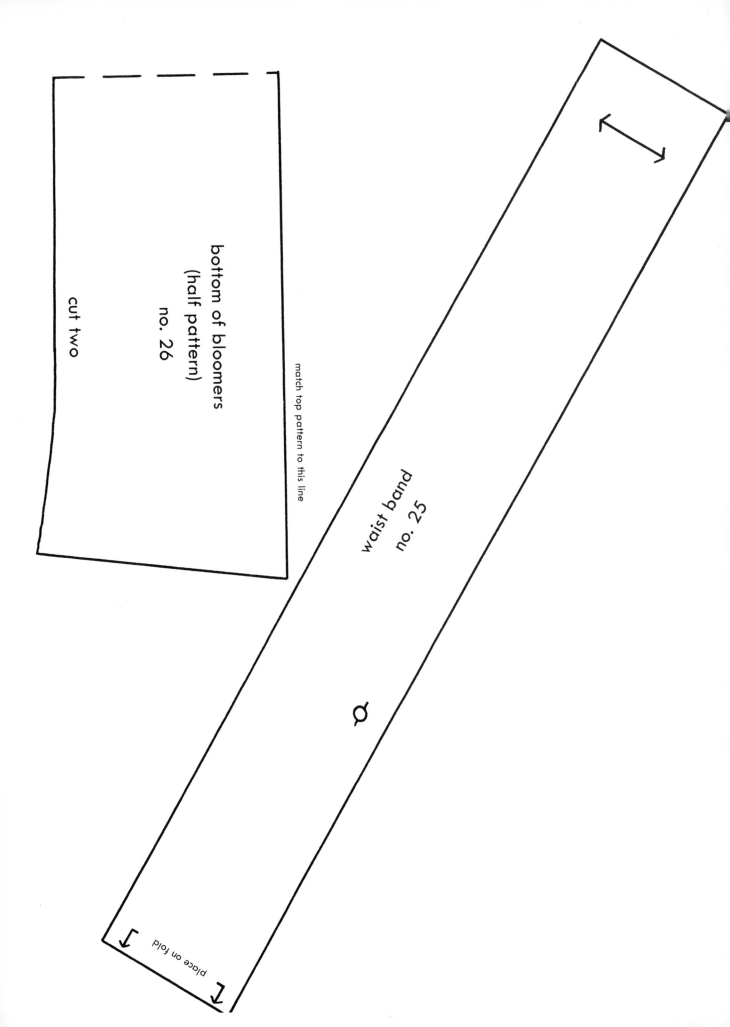

bottom of bloomers
(half pattern)
no. 26

cut two

match top pattern to this line

waist band
no. 25

place on fold

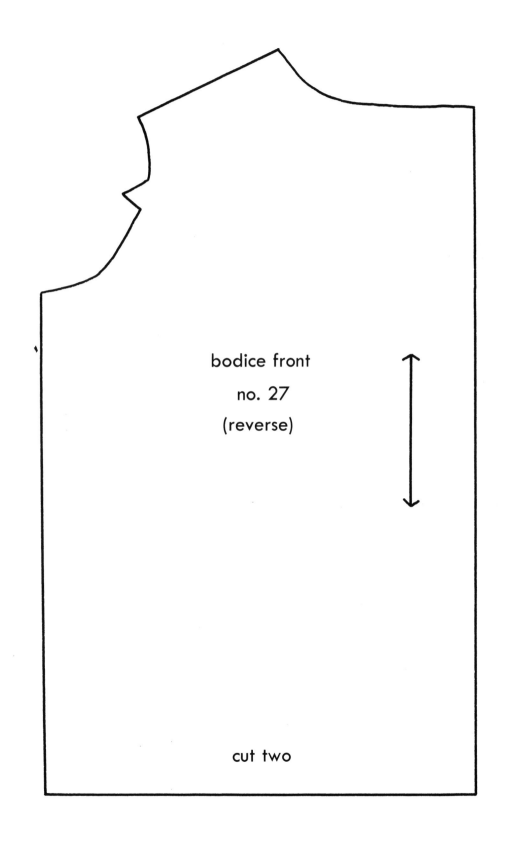

bodice front

no. 27

(reverse)

cut two

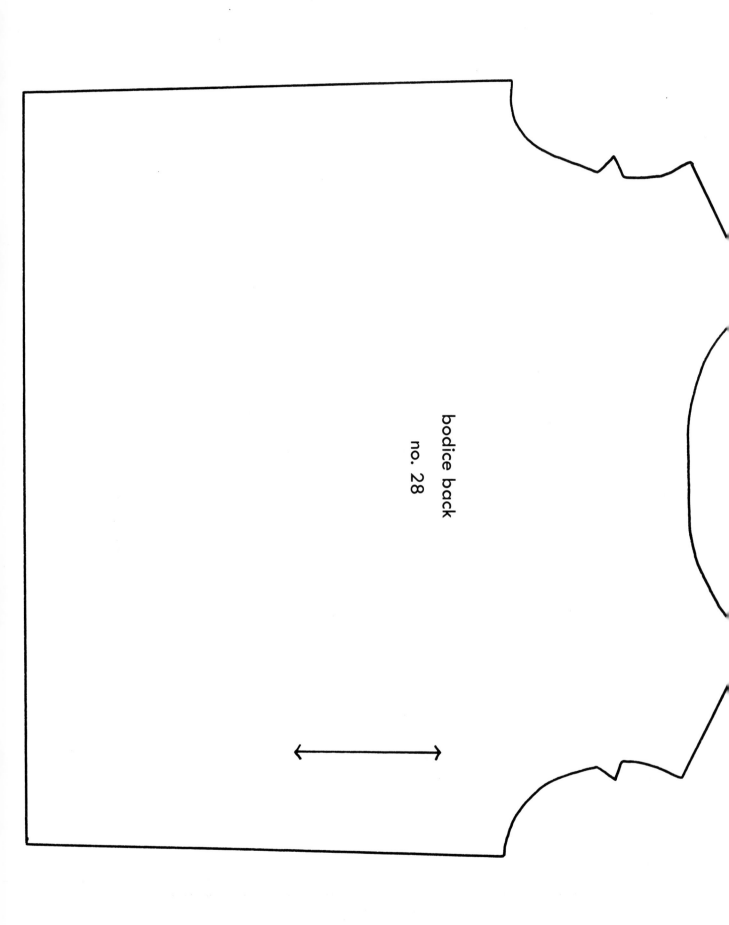

bodice back
no. 28

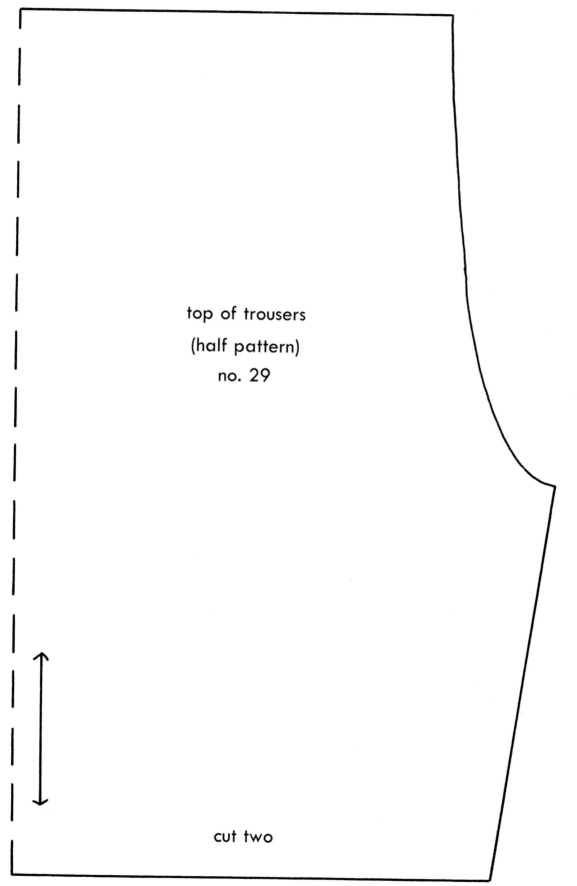

top of trousers

(half pattern)

no. 29

cut two

match bottom pattern to this line

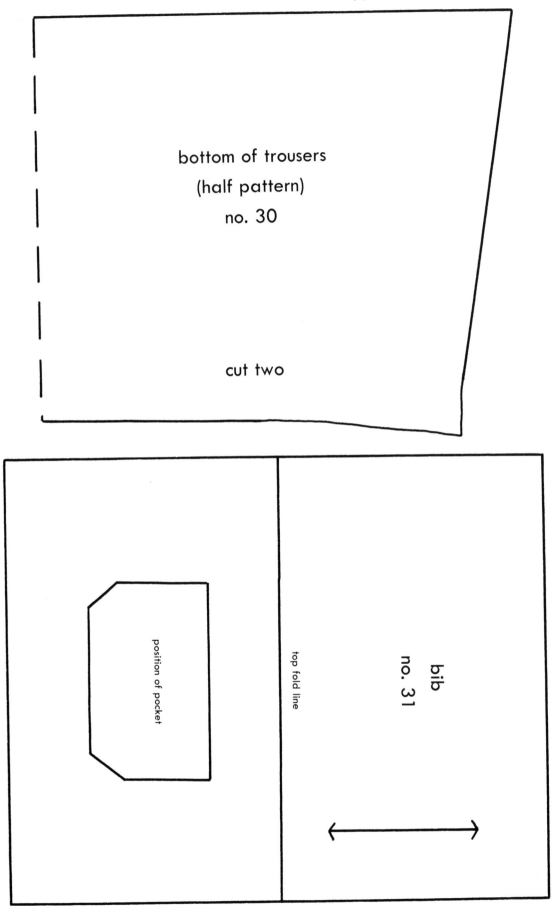

match top pattern to this line

bottom of trousers
(half pattern)
no. 30

cut two

position of pocket

top fold line

bib
no. 31

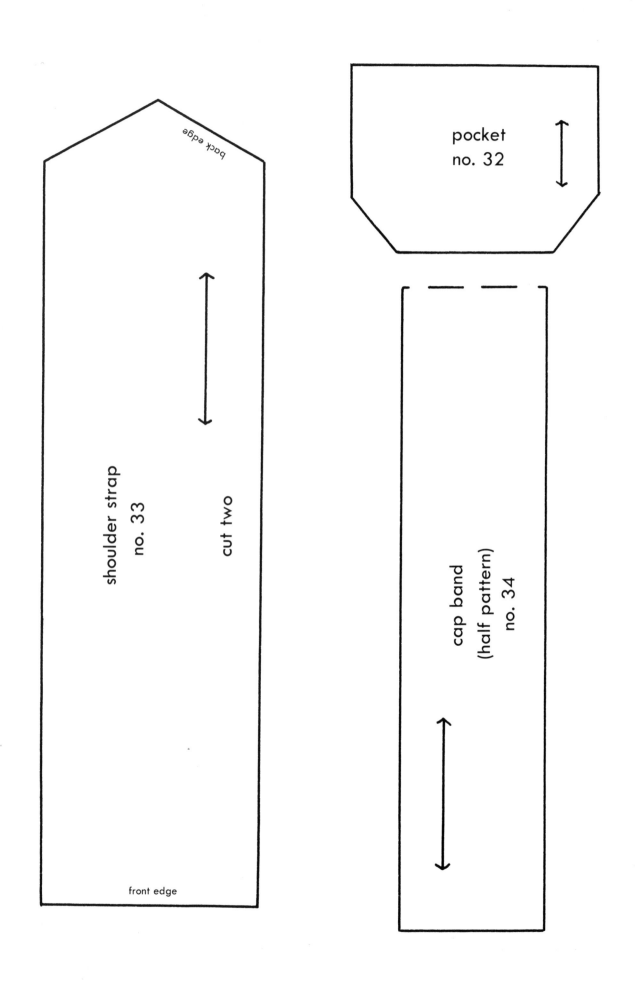

pocket
no. 32

shoulder strap

no. 33

cut two

back edge

front edge

cap band
(half pattern)
no. 34

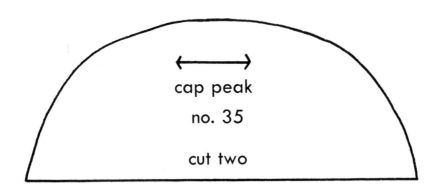

cap peak

no. 35

cut two

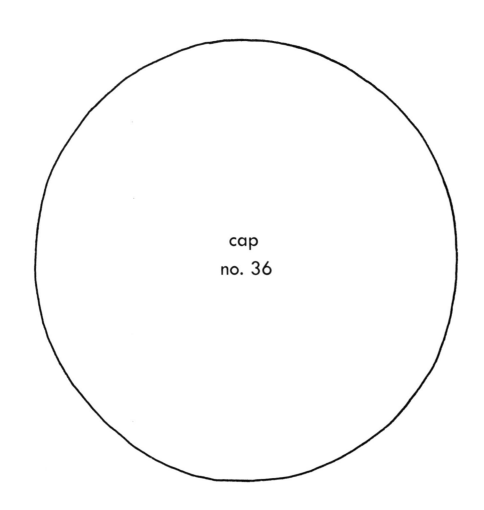

cap

no. 36

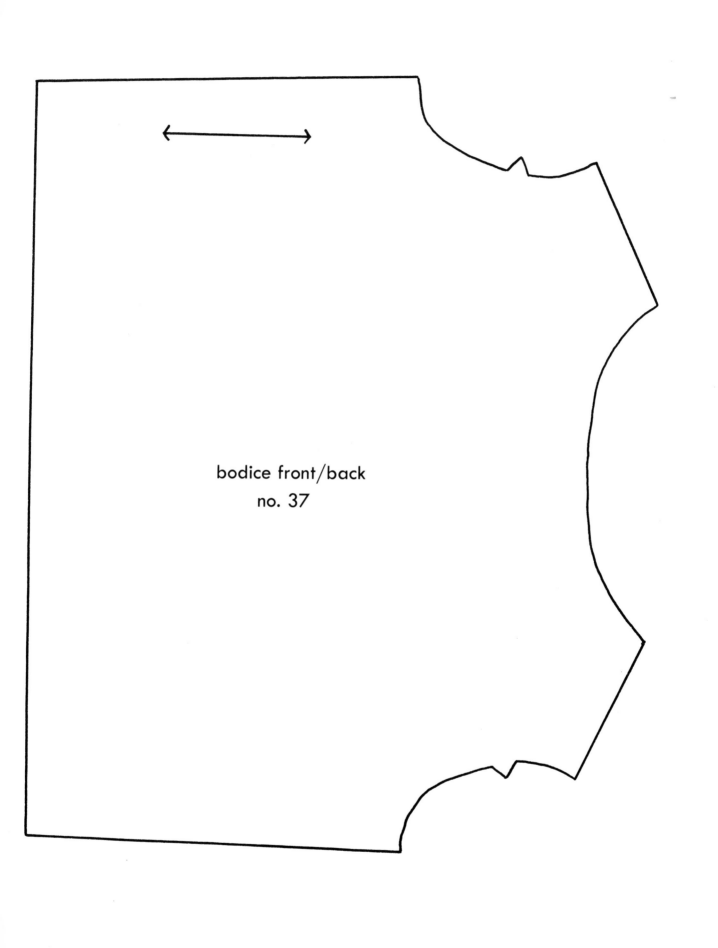

bodice front/back
no. 37

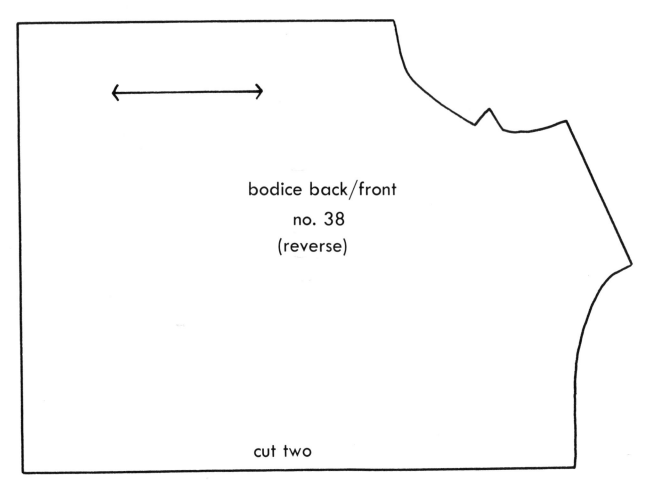

bodice back/front

no. 38

(reverse)

cut two

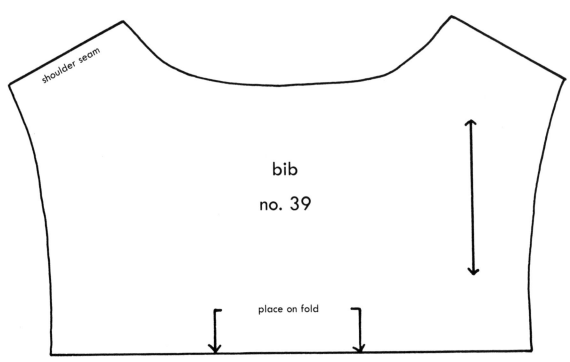

shoulder seam

bib

no. 39

place on fold

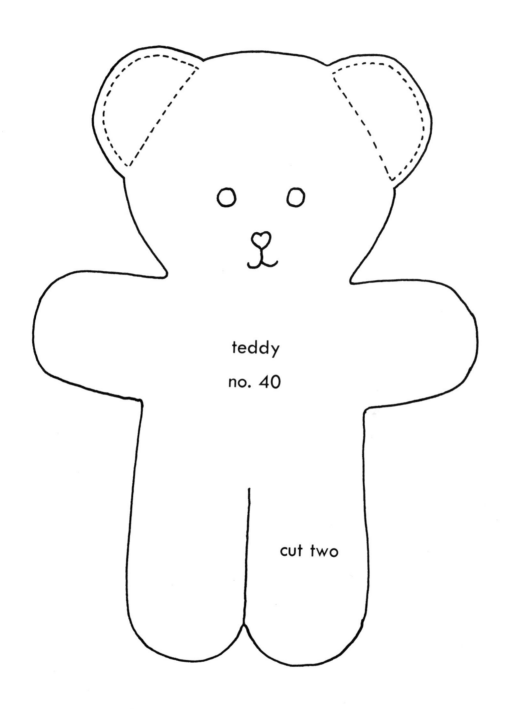

teddy

no. 40

cut two

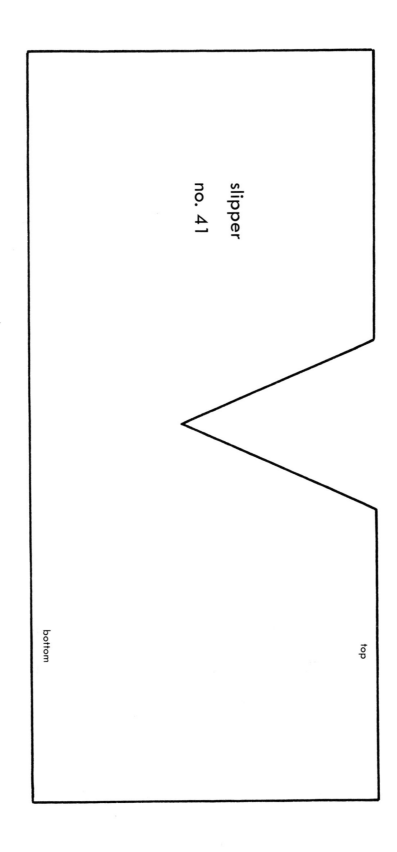

slipper
no. 41

bottom

top

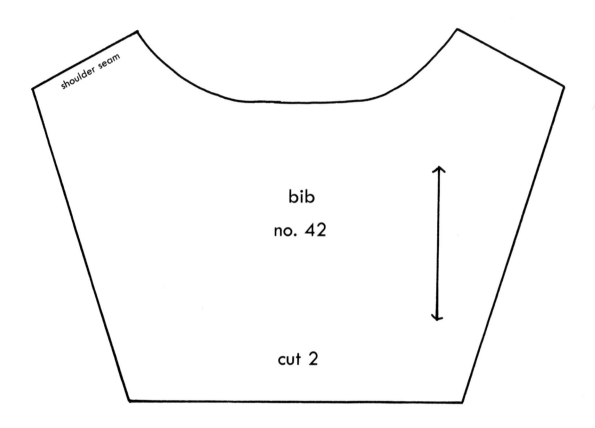

shoulder seam

bib

no. 42

cut 2

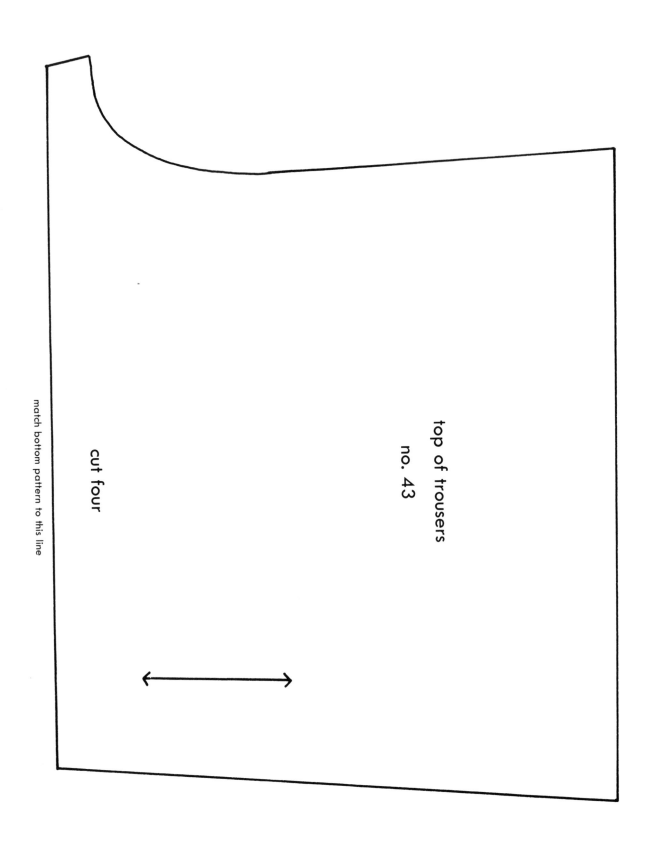

top of trousers
no. 43

cut four

match bottom pattern to this line

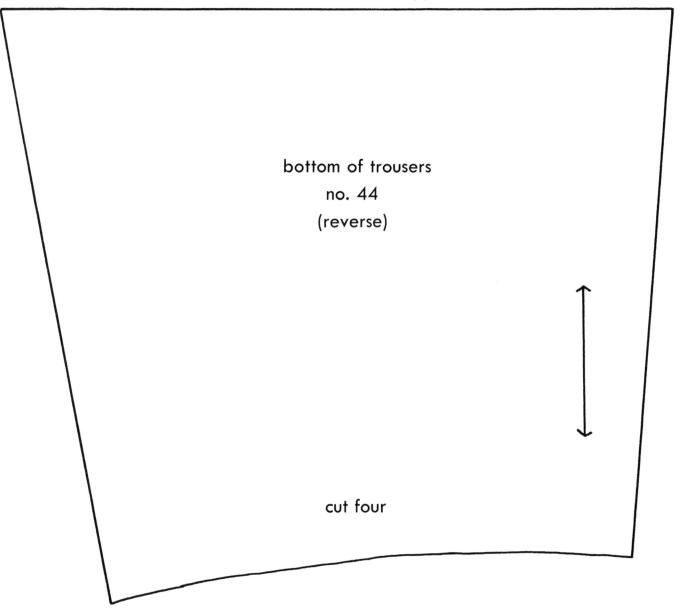

match top pattern to this line

bottom of trousers

no. 44

(reverse)

cut four

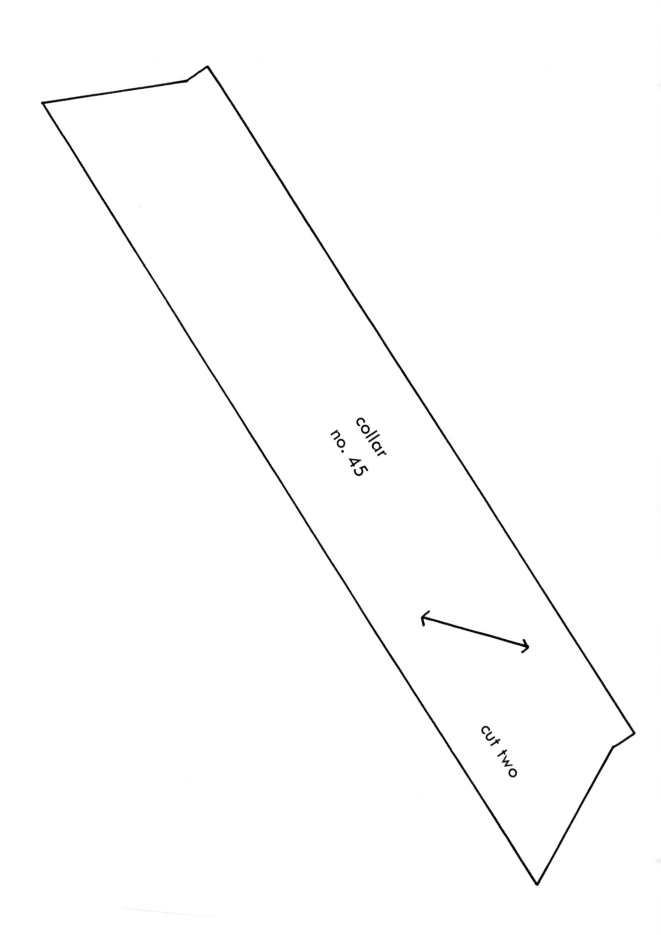

collar
no. 45

cut two

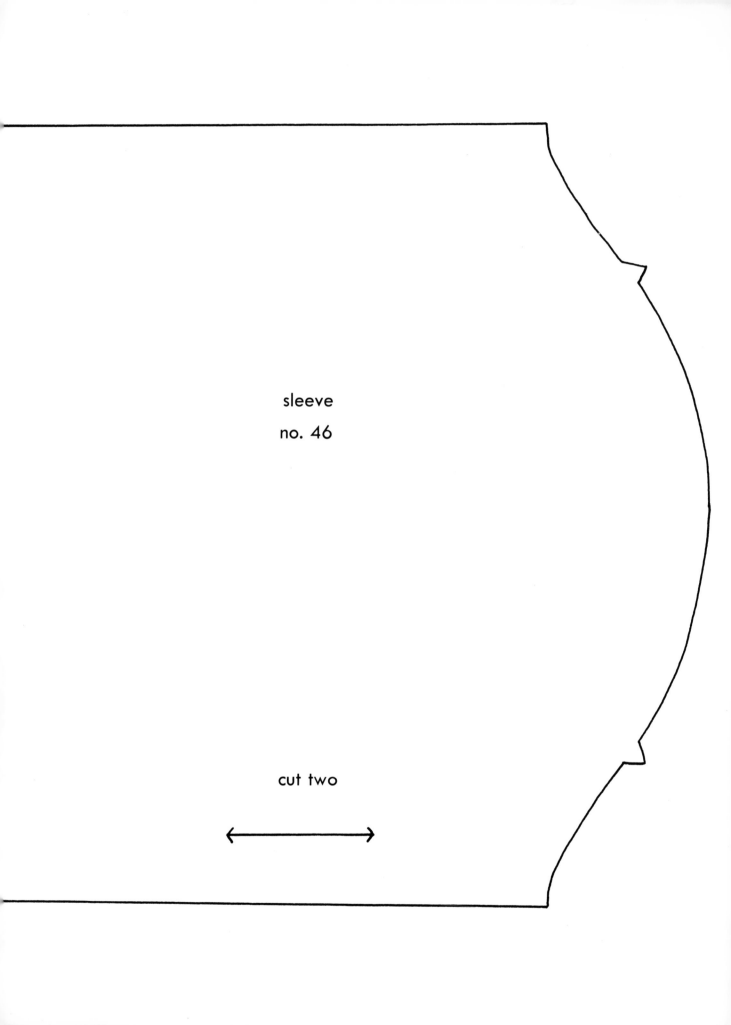

sleeve

no. 46

cut two

←——————→

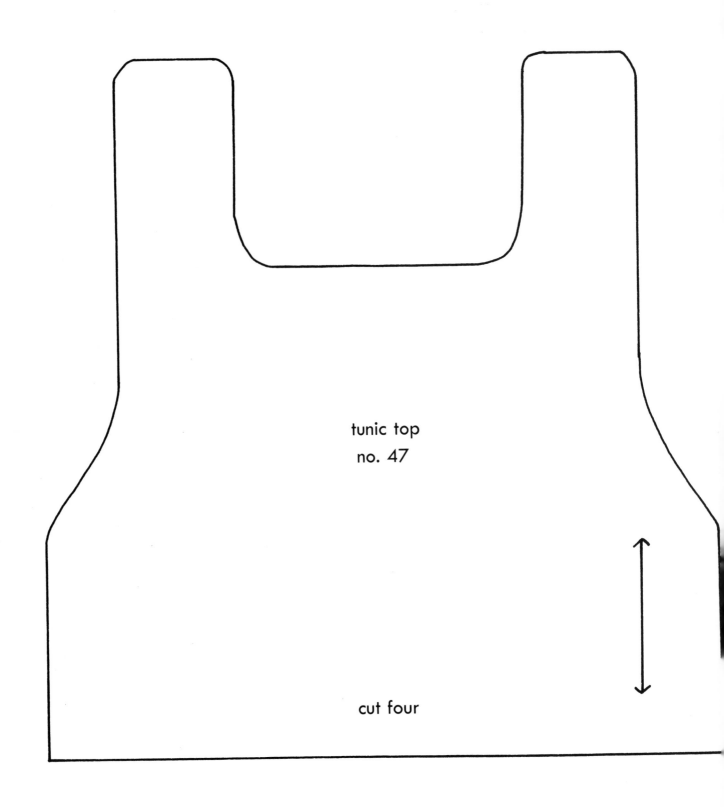

tunic top
no. 47

cut four

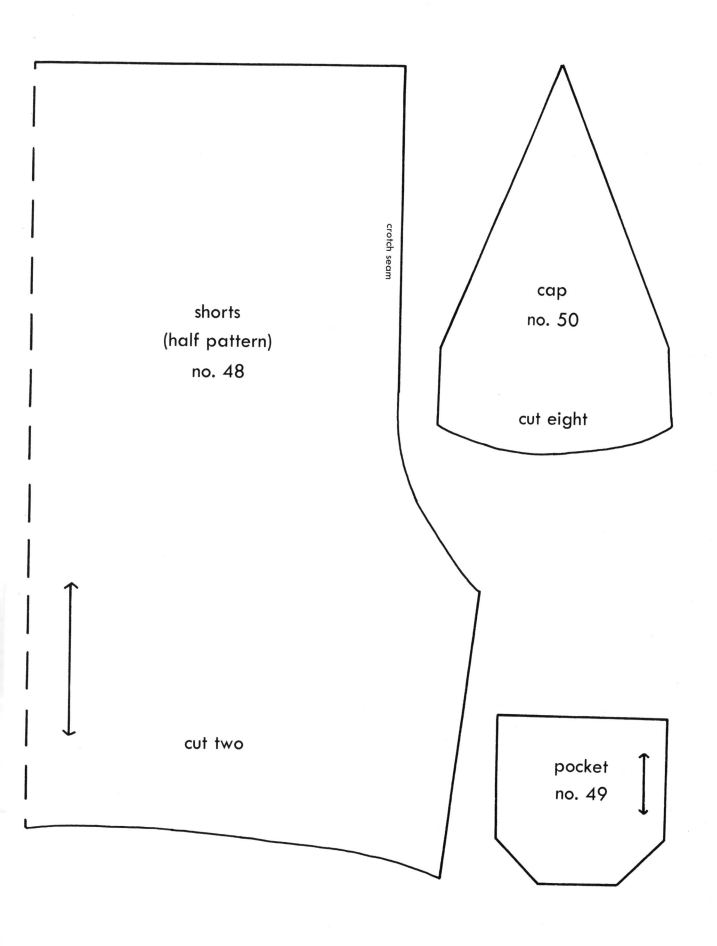

shorts
(half pattern)
no. 48

cut two

crotch seam

cap
no. 50

cut eight

pocket
no. 49

cap peak

no. 51

cut two

bottom of trousers

(half pattern)

no. 52

cut two

match top pattern to this line

shoulder strap

no. 53

cut two

back edge

front edge

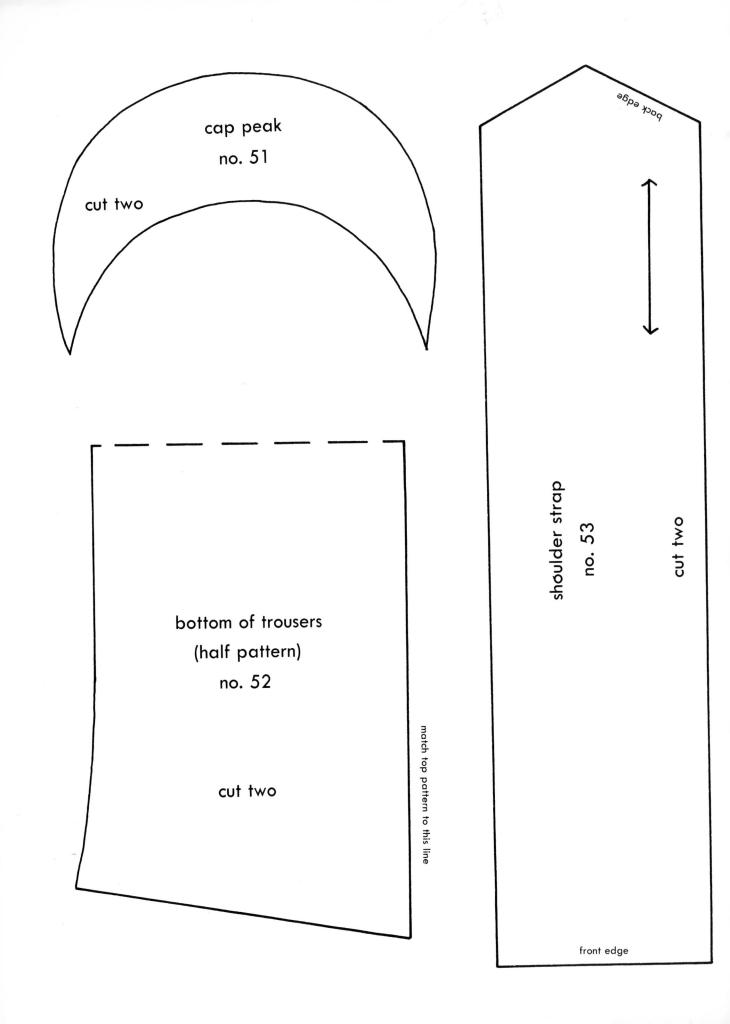

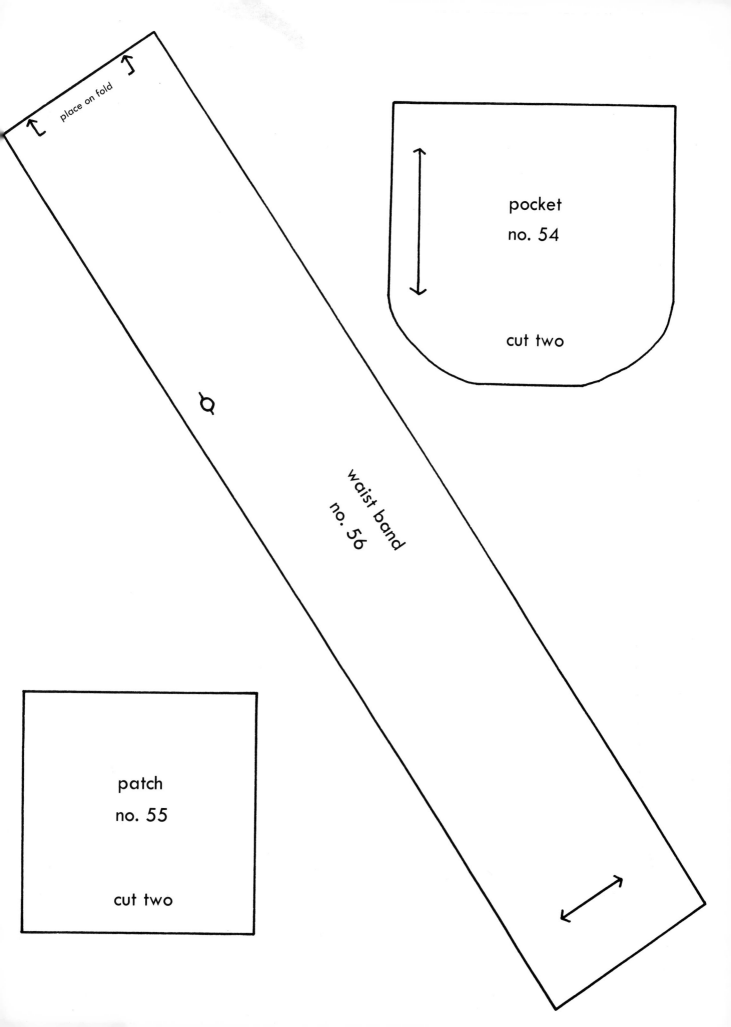

place on fold

waist band
no. 56

pocket
no. 54

cut two

patch
no. 55

cut two

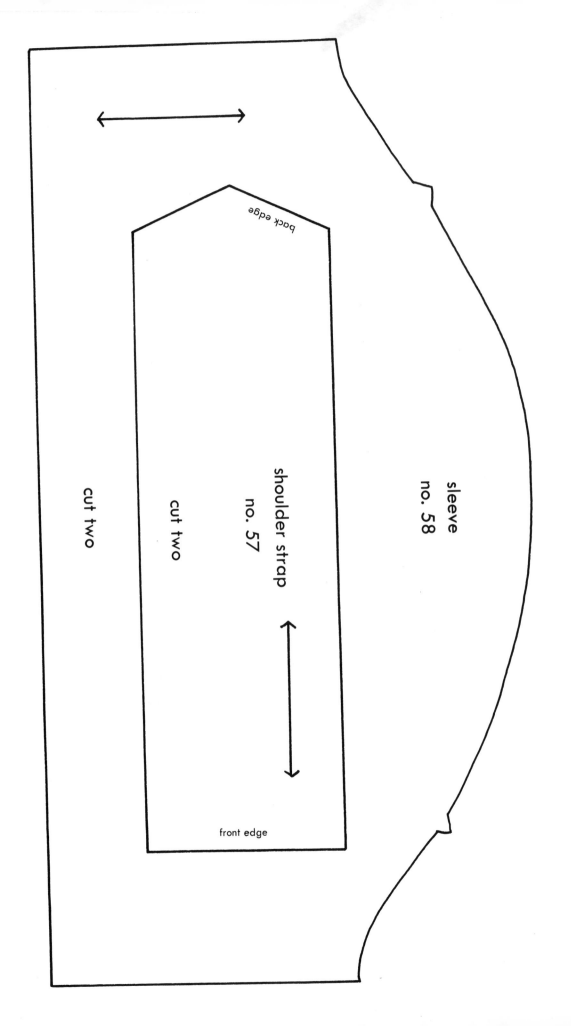

sleeve
no. 58

back edge

shoulder strap
no. 57

cut two

cut two

front edge

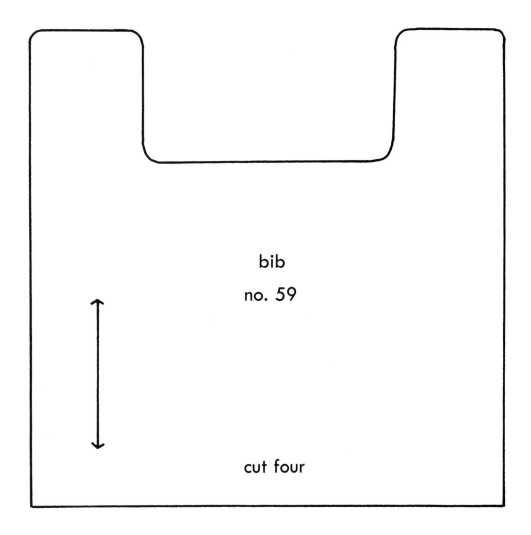

bib

no. 59

cut four

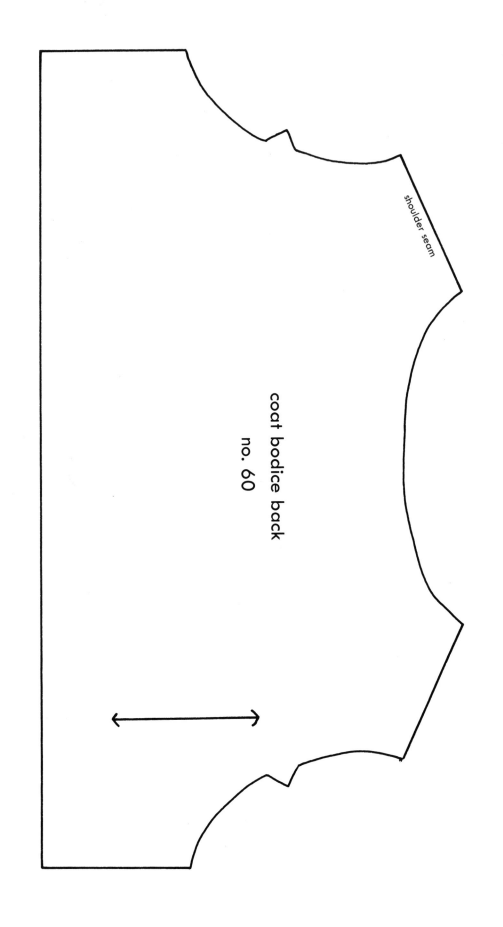

shoulder seam

coat bodice back
no. 60

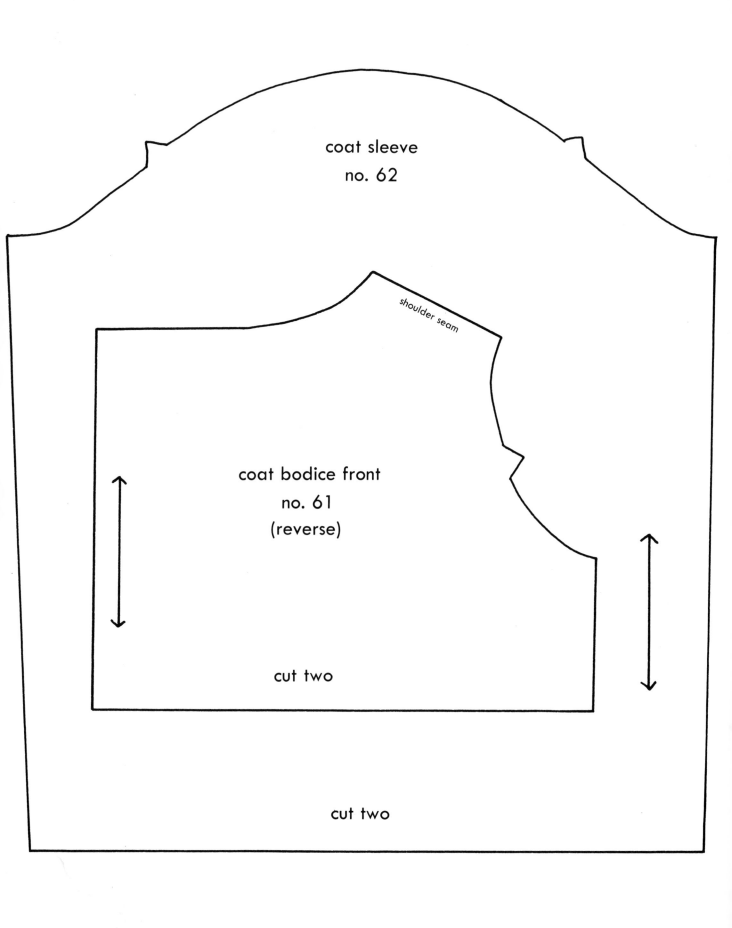

coat sleeve
no. 62

shoulder seam

coat bodice front
no. 61
(reverse)

cut two

cut two

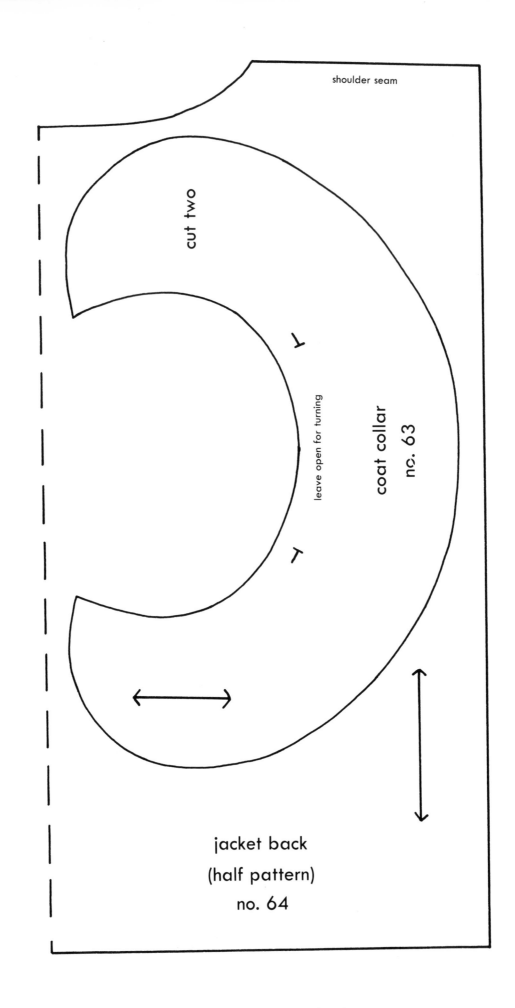

shoulder seam

cut two

leave open for turning

coat collar
no. 63

jacket back
(half pattern)
no. 64

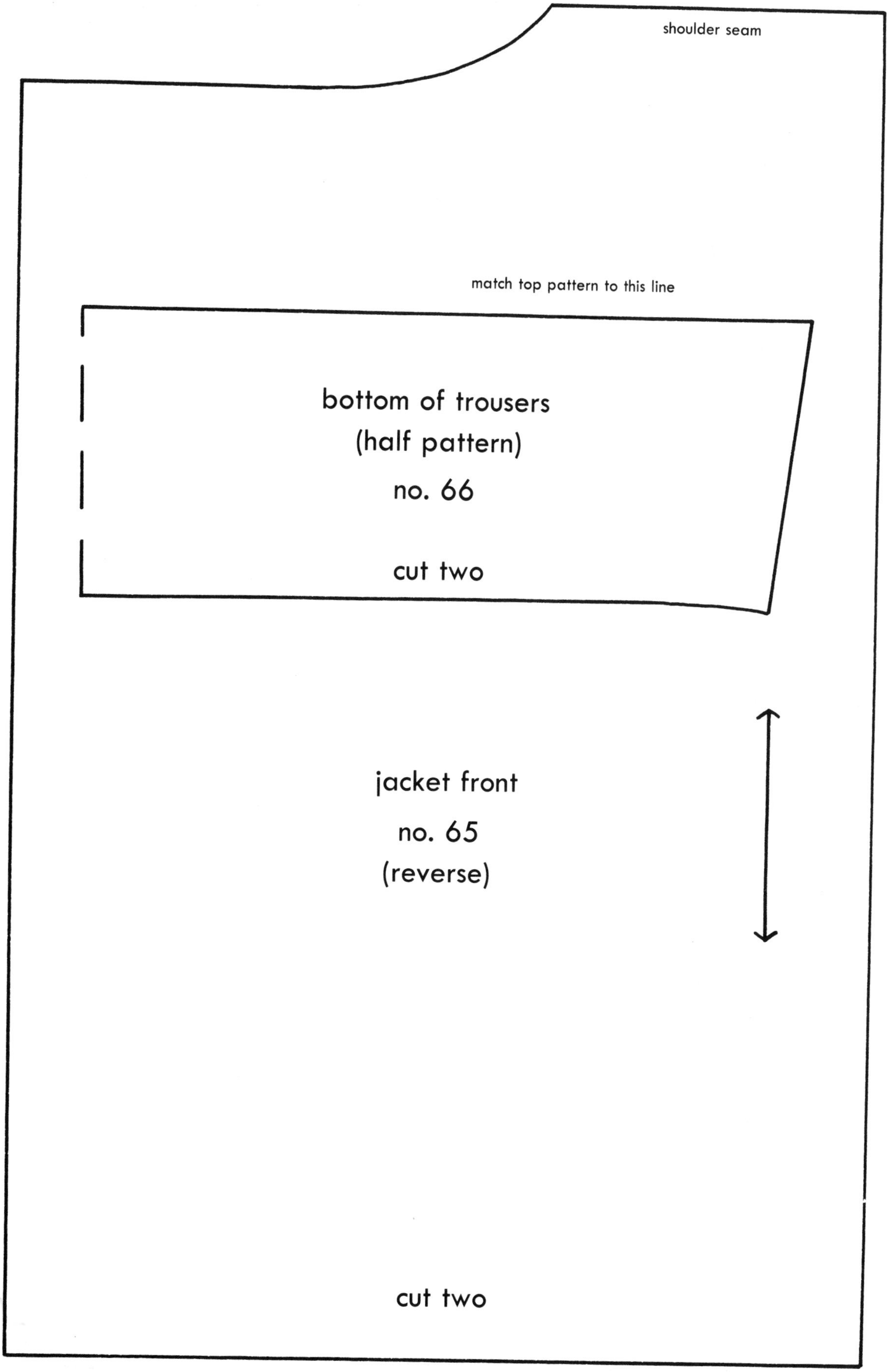

shoulder seam

match top pattern to this line

bottom of trousers
(half pattern)

no. 66

cut two

jacket front

no. 65
(reverse)

cut two

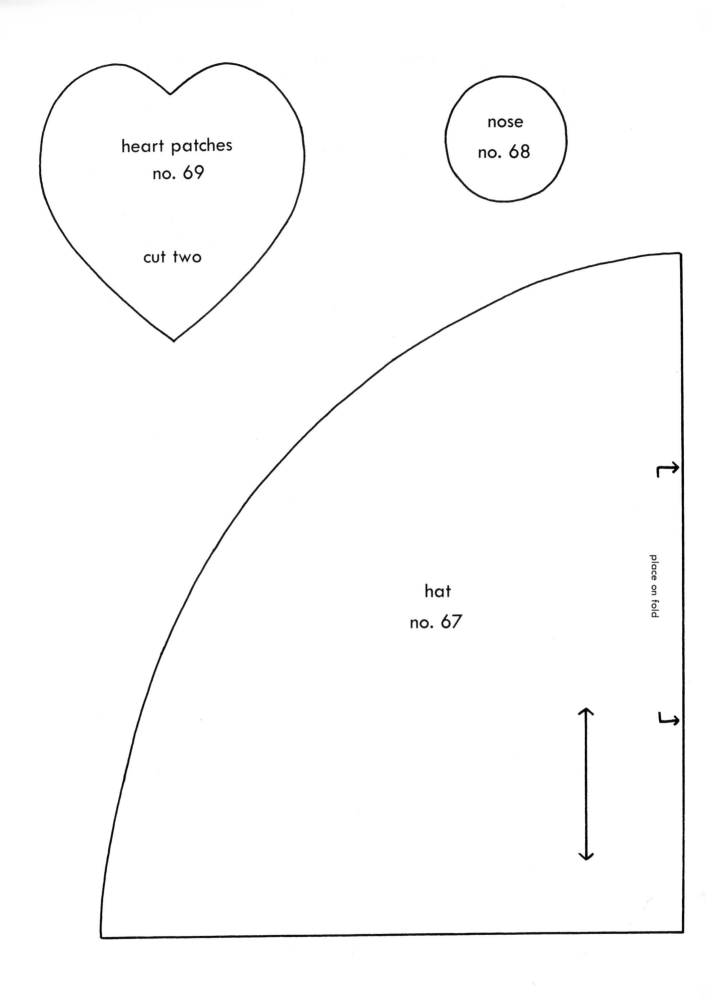

heart patches
no. 69

cut two

nose
no. 68

hat
no. 67

place on fold

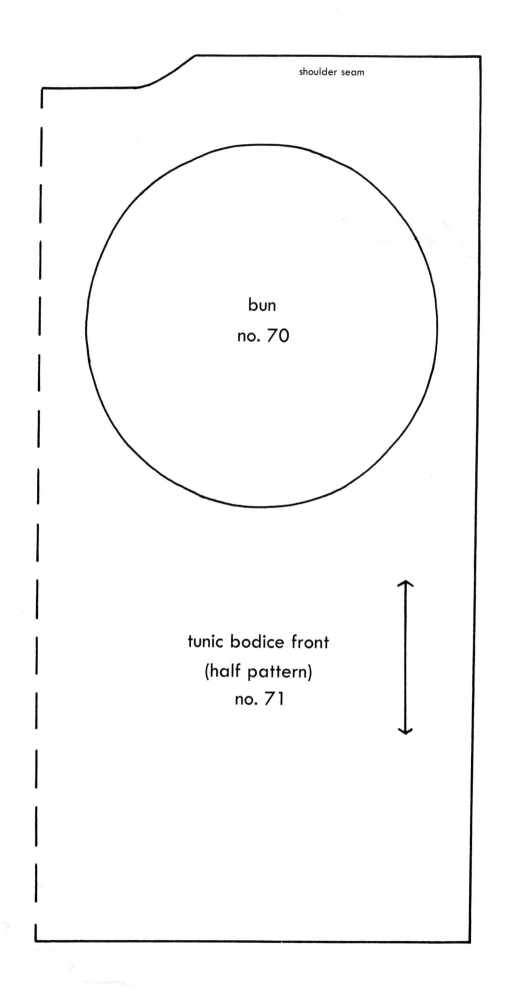

shoulder seam

bun
no. 70

tunic bodice front
(half pattern)
no. 71

shoulder seam

tunic bodice back

no. 72

(reverse)

cut two

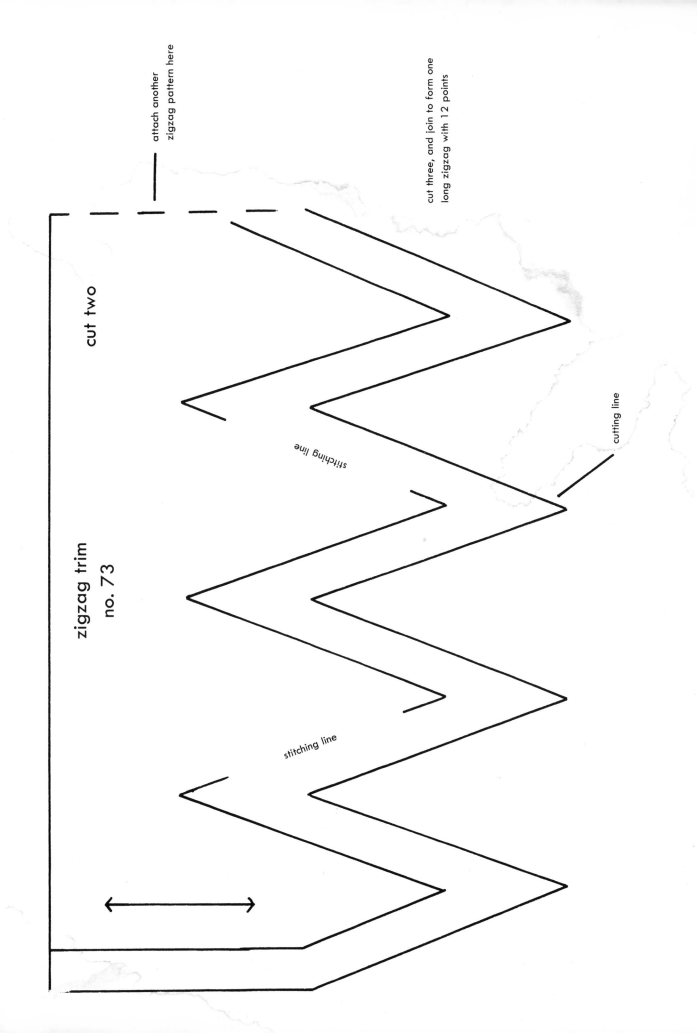

zigzag trim
no. 73

cut two

attach another
zigzag pattern here

cut three, and join to form one
long zigzag with 12 points

stitching line

stitching line

cutting line

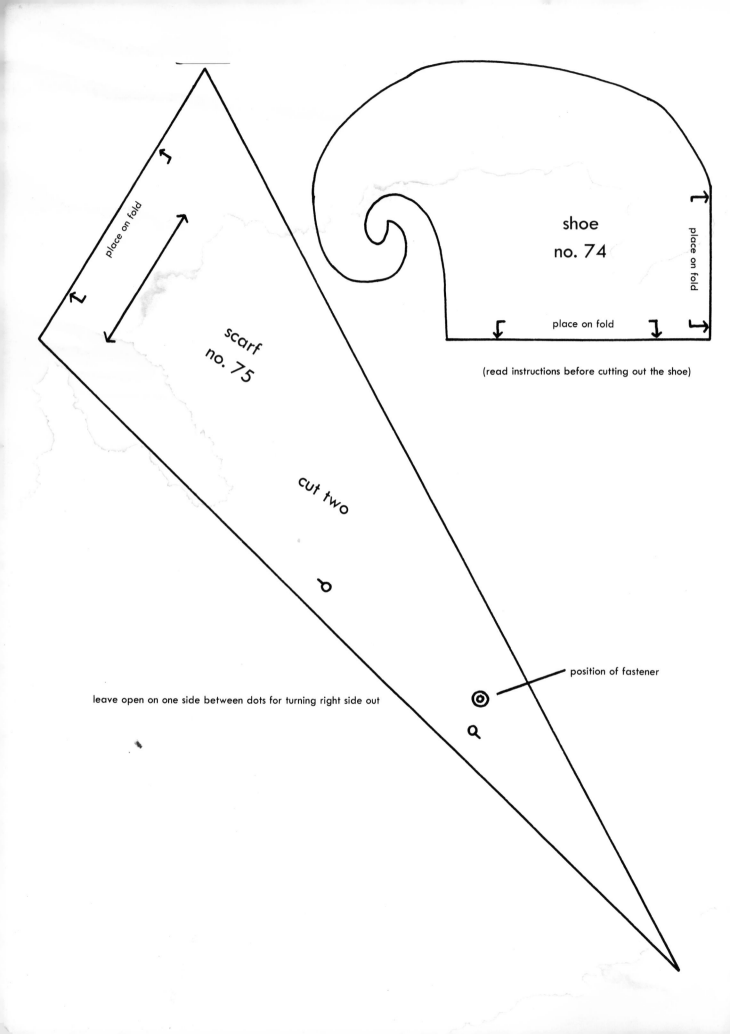

place on fold

scarf
no. 75

cut two

leave open on one side between dots for turning right side out

shoe
no. 74

place on fold

place on fold

(read instructions before cutting out the shoe)

position of fastener